Set-Jetting in Style

Leopard, Kruger National Park, South Africa.

Entrance to Angkor Thom, Cambodia

Set-Jetting in Style

Dr. Jill Nash and Carlo Nash

Jetty, Lake Windermere, Lake District.

Introduction

Some travellers will trek high mountains or spend serious money in casinos just because they watched a film featuring their favourite actor, be it Harrison Ford, Sean Connery or Brad Pitt. Travellers may aspire to that particular lifestyle or are captured by the fantasy of their favourite film, and just travelling to the location, seeing where it was filmed and where their favourite actors 'hung-out' makes the dream feel real. Set-Jetting in Style, is a book ideally suited to independent travellers who are fanatical about film. But this is not just a film reference book – it is also a travel guide.

We decided to publish this book because we too had been inspired to travel after watching films – not only did we want to visit film locations, but we wanted to soak up the local culture that had been captivated by cinema and stay in secret places where the stars had stayed. But of course we haven't featured the usual destinations in this guide – we've highlighted a mixture of local and 'off the beaten track' places that you wouldn't have thought we're used as film sets. Filmmakers have often used alternative film locations due to practical or budgetary restrictions, so this book highlights the unsung locations, such as Canada, which was used to film action blockbuster X-men.

Some destinations have been literally penned on the global map because of a major blockbuster hit. One that springs to mind was Cambodia following the launch of 'Lara Croft: Tomb Raider'. Tourism in Siem Reap literally rocketed overnight following the release of this film, and the press attention its starlet Angelina Jolie gave the country. This is no bad thing, providing travelers act and travel responsibly.

'Set-Jetting in Style' is our third book in the Luxury Backpackers series – this book features detailed coverage of our favourite 'must see' films, from different genres such as action and adventure to musicals. We hope you enjoy reading this book as much as we've enjoyed researching it – and it inspires you to travel and explore the globe.

Jill & Carlo

What kind of Set-Jetter
are you?

● Action + Adventure   ● Musicals

● Science Fiction   ● Romantic Comedy

Crime + Gangster

Epics + Historical

I must start by saying travel is one of my favourite pastimes. I am lucky to travel all over the world through my work in the past as a musician, and for the last 15 years or so as an actor, and I feel it really is one of the most important things a person can do if you are interested in growing spiritually. The gift of travel and our planes, trains and automobiles really is a fantastic one. 24 hours to Australia; 10 hours to LA; 14 hours and you are in the most beautiful surroundings that is the Maldives.

Since the age of 18 when I first started travelling on tour with Paul Weller and the 'Brand New Heavies' I have had the luxury of nearly travelling all over the world! Brazil and China being the only 2 places I've not visited. To experience the different cultures around the world is such an invaluable asset to have and one I will strongly advise my children to follow if I have any!

From the politeness and succinctness of the Far East to the warmth of Ireland, there is a new lesson to be learned on how to enjoy life, and embrace everything it has to offer if you're a nomad like me!

Films have a major influence on our subconscious, we all know how excited we get when, if for example your walking down Wilshire Blvd in LA and someone points out Kate Mantilini's diner and says "Hey that's where they shot 'Heat' with De Niro" and walking along the coastline of Ireland marvelling at the site of Ryan's daughter. Film is as magical as some of the exotic places it has created, and I like others, venture out to find them after seeing a movie.

One example is Cliveden in Taplow Berkshire as shown in the movie Scandal. This place is historical and beautiful, and you feel a real sense of magic as you saunter down that long drive way, with history beckoning you with its teasing little finger. Le Manoir aux Quat'Saisons is another place of escapism and magic for me. Venturing out into Europe 'The Marbella club' is somewhere I always go to de-stress or write. I'm just finishing my screenplay for Mr Goodnight and to find a place this time of the year that has the fine weather and great service can be hard. The Marbella club is the greatest! Of all the places in the world though, my favourite has to be the Maldives. Real white beaches, clear turquoise seas its simply stunning. I have no doubt that every magazine covers depicting white sands at their resorts are in fact secretly the Maldives. Kanuhura Island is one of my favourite places to stay. Enjoy the book but most importantly get out there in the world. There is so much to see!

Max Beesley
Actor

Le Manoir aux Quat'Saisons.

Chatsworth House © Pathe Images.

UNITED KINGDOM

Scotland + Northumberland | North West |
Peak District | London

North Sea

North Atlantic
Ocean

Edinburgh

Durham

Liverpool ● Manchester

Ireland

★ London

English Channel

🏆 Why is this place so special?

The United Kingdom of Great Britain and Northern Island (commonly known as the UK) maybe a small island country – but is packed full of ancient sites, fabulous countryside, historical cities and of course home to world famous football teams.

England accounts for just over half of the total area of the UK, Scotland about a third, Wales about a tenth, while Northern Island covers just 14,000sq.kms. England mostly consists of lowland terrain, with mountainous terrain in the north such as the Cumbrian Mountains of the Lake District, and the Pennines of the Peak District. England's highest mountain is Scafell Pike, located in the Lake District, and is a popular tourist destination for locals and foreigners due its picturesque scenery, great lakes and countryside culture. England has a number of historical cities, including its vibrant capital London, which attracts millions of tourists a year to visit the famous palaces, gardens and crown jewels. However, Manchester and Liverpool which have undergone considerable regeneration projects over recent years are increasingly popular due to the lively music scenes and legendary football stadiums.

Scotland consists of nearly 800 islands notably the Hebrides, Orkney Islands and Shetland Islands and its topography is distinguished by the Highland Boundary Fault which traverses the Scottish mainland from Helensburgh to Stonehaven. Due to these mountainous areas Scotland is a destination renowned for the great outdoors with hiking, canoeing and famously the 'highland games' attracting tourism. Scotland also has an abundance of national heritage, famed for its whisky production, musical bagpipes and its stunning capital Edinburgh, which is home to the New Years Eve party 'Hogmanay'.

Wales maybe renowned for its myths, legends and dragons – but there is far more to this highly spirited nation. Its cosmopolitan capital Cardiff is a stunning city with a lively waterfront and castle to boot. Llandudno is Wales' largest resort town and

has turned quickly into a hip weekend destination
for urbanites. Not to mention the Pembrokeshire
Coast National Park home to gorgeous beaches
and surfing schools.

Northern Ireland's capital Belfast, maybe
famed for the city that built the 'Titanic' – but
Northern Ireland is equally renowned for its
stunning scenery, the impressive Giants Causeway
and coastal routes, it's traditional folk music and,
of course, the Irish pub.

The United Kingdom has been pretty
influential in the development of cinema, with
Ealing Studios claiming to be the oldest studio
in the world. Despite a history of important
and successful productions, the industry is
characterised by an ongoing debate about its
identity, and the influences of American and
European cinema. Though the popularity of British
films have certainly stirred an awakening in British
tourism, in particular historical sites such as
Alnwick castle (which was used as a film set for
Harry Potter), have become tourist hits overnight.
The UK is universally renowned however for
producing independent and epic films, perhaps due
to the hundreds of years of history, its prevailing
monarchy, and sites such as Chatsworth House,
Buckingham Palace and Edinburgh castle which
still stand proudly today.

📖 Fast Facts

Capital: London.

Location: Western Europe, surrounded by
the English Channel, Atlantic Ocean, North
Sea and Irish Sea.

Population: 61 million.

Religion: Christianity 71%, Islam 2.8%,
Hinduism 1%, other 26.1%.

Languages: The two official languages are
English and Welsh, English being the most
widely spoken. Scottish Gaelic is also spoken
in some parts of Scotland.

Getting there and exploring around

It is easy to travel to the UK. There are flights to London, Manchester and Edinburgh from most parts of the world. You can travel around the UK by train and bus, although the services are not known for being very efficient. There are regional train companies such as TransPennine trains (which run across the north east) which are a bit more reliable or try the luxurious Orient Express if you feel like splashing out - which runs day and weekend breaks across the UK such as The Edinburgh Tattoo weekend or afternoon tea to the Lake District.

Alternatively it is pretty easy to hire a car for a weekend, using one of the many national car hire companies or rent a bike for the day if you're not travelling far, or even enjoy a 'ramble' in the national parks.

As the country is quite small, it is easy to make day-trips to other parts of Britain. The UK is close to the many different countries of continental Europe (such as France, Germany, Belgium) and is linked to France by the channel tunnel, which makes it convenient to access the rest of mainland Europe by train (known as the Eurostar). Lille and Paris are just a couple of hours away which are popular routes for day trips.

There are also internal flights from the northern airports to London (as well as Scotland) so depending on the time you have, and your location (if you're the other side of London for example it could take you a good 2 hours to get to Heathrow!) it may make sense to fly.

Best time of year to visit

The United Kingdom has a temperate climate, with plentiful rainfall all year round (!). The temperature varies with the seasons but seldom drops below −10°C or rises above 35°C. The UK generally doesn't suffer from extremes. Atlantic currents, warmed by the Gulf Stream, bring mild winters, especially in the west, where winters are wet, especially over high ground. Summers are warmest in the south east of England, being closest to the European mainland, and coolest in the north. Snowfall can occur in winter and early spring, though it rarely settles to great depth away from high ground.

The best time to visit the UK is generally between July to September as the climate usually warm making sightseeing more pleasurable and there any many music festivals (such as the famous Glastonbury) and summer parties. Although Spring (April – May) is equally stunning as flowers (such as bluebells and daffodils) begin to grow and lambs are born which makes it an enjoyable time to visit the many national parks.

❓ Must know before you go

Bring a brolly. The UK is renowned for its unpredictable climate and taking an umbrella wherever you go, whatever the weather, is a must.

Public transport. It's renowned for being slow and unreliable. So don't trust it if you have to get anywhere on time – take a taxi, ride a bike or hire a car.

Queuing. British people are generally polite and courteous and love to queue. Queue jumping is frown upon – wait in line and wait for your turn.

📷 Highlights

Scottish steam train. The scenery across the Glenfinnan viaduct is breathtaking. The traditional Scottish steam train takes you back in history.

Derbyshire in style. Spend a day at Chatsworth House, exploring the stunning grounds and admiring the ancient architecture, which was used for many period dramas before munching on a delicious champagne afternoon tea.

Hiking in the Lake District. Rambling in the Cumbrian hills and admiring the scenery with a backpack picnic is a pure delight; whatever the weather.

London in love. Spend an evening in London walking the romantic locations from films such as Shakespeare in Love, Bridget Jones Diary or grab an evening coffee in the literary district of Notting Hill.

⭐ Star Spotting

Head to the traditional English pub 'Punch Bowl' set in the back streets of Mayfair (London) for a night schmoozing with local film director Guy Ritchie (who apparently owns a share of the pub). Other high profile celebrities including Robert De Niro are also rumoured to have paid a visit here.

Genre: Action + Adventure
Destination: Scotland + Northumberland

✈ Regional Information

Scotland is a heartfelt country, rich in history and beautiful countryside. Famous for its clans, kilts, medieval castles, as well as poetry and festivals. Its fresh water lochs (lakes) expand over 600 sq. miles – notably the most famous being Loch Ness where a mysterious monster is said to lurk in the depths of the water; and has been the subject of children's' programmes, stories and films for years.

Theatre lovers from around the world flock to its capital, Edinburgh (which was also built on 7 hills like Rome, Italy) for its famous street theatres and annual 'Fringe' festival as well as the spirited 'Hogmanay', which is the lively New Years eve party that covers the entire city with live bands, fireworks from the castle and men dancing in kilts playing bagpipes. The stunning Loch Lomond region, which crosses both highland and lowland, has the largest surface area of fresh water in the UK. The area has plenty of charming villages and pleasant hostelries which fringe the loch's shores, such as Drymen, with its many popular bays and viewpoints. It's no wonder it attracts so many visitors, and why it's such a popular filming location.

Scotland is incredibly easy to get around, with so many things to see such as visit castles, gardens, whisky distilleries or for the more energetic, hiking, skiing, white water rafting or embark in a game of golf.

Dividing Scotland and England is Hadrian's Wall, spanning 84 miles, built by the Roman empire, which today is south of Scotland's political border and 90% of Northumberland is actually north of the wall. The wall itself crosses Cumbria, the Pennines and Tynside which makes it popular for fell walkers – walking the 'coast to coast' trail. Northumberland, which is home to Alnwick and the historic town 'Berwick upon tweed', is popular for its castles (Alnwick, Bamburgh, Dunstanburgh and Warkworth) sandy beaches and little hamlets. Today, Northumberland is still largely rural, and the least populated county in England. In recent years the county has had considerable growth in tourism due to its scenic beauty and the abundant evidence of history.

Genre: Action + Adventure
Destination: Scotland + Northumberland

Harry Potter and the Chamber of Secrets (2002)

There aren't many films that capture the imagination of children worldwide that can rival the 'Harry Potter' series. The books originally made their debut onto screen for the first novel 'The Philosophers stone' in 2001, and the book series in total has sold more than 400 million copies worldwide, with the initial 4 titles selling faster than any book in history. So the Harry Potter series in undoubtedly popular – not just with children but equally with adults.

'The chamber of secrets' sees Harry and his friends returning to Hogwarts school of witchcraft and wizardry for their second year. Whilst a number of locations in the UK were used to produce the second film such as Gloucester Cathedral, Oxford University and Kings Cross station – the producers decided on the more scenic locations of the north east of England and Scotland to depict the backdrop for Hogwarts and Harry's adventures.

In the opening scenes Harry and Ron drive the battered Ford Anglia car which lands on Glenfinnan Viaduct, on the West Highland line between Fort William and Mallaig in Scotland. If you want to cross the viaduct in a traditional steam locomotive, West Coast Railways run the Jacobite Steam Train during the summer season. The dramatic landscapes around Hogwarts were filmed in the area of Glencoe, using the stunning backdrops of the lakes, woodland and mountainous scenery.

On Harry's arrival at Hogwarts the producers used the scenic Alnwick castle in Northumberland for the entrance scenes, which has since become a bit of an institution (and subsequently organizes Harry Potter tours of the set).

Durham Cathedral provides internal shots of Hogwarts, the Chapter House becomes the classroom in which Professor McGonagall teaches the young wizards to transform animals into water goblets.

Stylish Place to Stay

Langley castle, Northumberland
Built in 1350, during the reign of Edward III, the castle has retained its architectural integrity and is regarded as one of the few medieval fortified Castle Hotels in England. The nineteen guest rooms, all with private facilities, are luxuriously appointed. Some have private features such as a four-poster bed and a window seat set in the 7ft thick castle walls, so you'll feel like you're really staying at Hogwarts! The location is situated in the Northumberland National Park – between Durham and Alnwick – which means you can explore both locations with relative ease.

Delicious Place to Eat

Lilburns, Alnwick
Situated on Paikes Lane down the cobbled street in Alnwick, with al fresco dining in the summer months. The proprietors Rod & Debbie offer a warm and friendly service in this contemporary, family run bistro serving a range of meals from a light bite to a full three courses. The restaurant is licensed and a full range of wines and beers are stocked.

Genre: Action + Adventure
Destination: Scotland + Northumberland

Braveheart (1995)

Braveheart tells the story of Scottish hero and legend William Wallace - played by Mel Gibson, who also produced and directed the film. Wallace, who gained recognition when he came to the forefront of the First War of Scottish Independence by opposing Edward I of England. The action/epic movie was produced with a solid cast, rousing battle scenes, using the backdrop of the Scottish Highlands – even though parts of the film were actually shot in Ireland. There is no denying that this film was a box office hit, even though film critics claim that Braveheart was historically inaccurate, it didn't stop it winning five Oscars in 1996.

The Scottish scenes were filmed in and around the stunning areas of Glencoe, Glen Nevis and the Mamore mountains. The landscapes could not be faked or emulated in a studio, thus providing a realistic and riveting setting.

The film's opening scenes were set in the village of 'Lanark', where the young Wallace grows up, and falls in love with Murron, which was constructed in the Glen Nevis Valley at the foot of Ben Nevis. Although the set was dismantled after filming and the area returned to its former state, the Braveheart Car Park has been retained.

As Wallace's legend grows he treks along the spectacular mountain path filmed on the Mamores, a group of ten mountains linked by a narrow ridge, stretching between Loch Leven itself and Glen Nevis. The interior of Mornay's castle was filmed in Edinburgh Council Chamber.

The film generated huge interest in Scotland and in Scottish history, not only around the world, but also within Scotland itself. Fans come from all over the world to see the places in Scotland where William Wallace fought for Scottish freedom – and to see the infamous statue of Wallace in Stirling, Scotland.

Stylish Place to Stay

The Winnock Hotel, Loch Lomond
This little gem rests in the heart of Loch Lomond National Park, offering historic charm, and friendly service. The Winnock Hotel surrounds the pretty village green in the centre of Drymen, on the east side of Loch Lomond. It is superbly situated for exploring the beautiful rustic countryside as well as the cities of central Scotland and not to mention the Glengoyne Whisky Distillery and Wallace monument which are relatively close by. It has been recently extensively refurbished and modernised, whilst retaining the 18th century character of the original inn.

Delicious Place to Eat

The Clachan Inn, Drymen
The Clachan Inn in Drymen by Loch Lomond is Scotland's oldest registered licensed premises (1734). It's a perfect stopping point if you're walking the West Highland way, and offers a couple of rooms B&B if you drink too much ale and need to stay the night! The Clachan Inn reeks with history and serves traditional Scottish home cooking.

Genre: Romantic Comedy
Destination: North West

✢ Regional Information

The North West is a diverse corner of England featuring energetic cities such as Manchester and Liverpool, the quaint countryside of Cheshire and the stunning mountainous area of the Cumbrian Lake District.

Although generally renowned as the 'wettest' area of Great Britain – due to the high levels of rainfall – this never dampens the spirit of local people. The North West is popular both for British tourists as a weekend getaway as well as international visitors due to the picturesque scenery and 'Englishness'. Poets, writers and painters for hundreds of years have all been inspired by the fells, pretty villages and wildlife – equally so have film directors.

The ambling paths of Cumbria's great outdoors are the perfect place for stress-busting or adrenaline-pumping. Watching the world go by from bustling coffee shops or get a different kind of buzz as you test your limits on a mountain bike or zip wire. Whether you're on a sedate stroll or scrambling along cliff faces, there are so many stunning views. England highest peak –'Scafell Pike' which lies at the foot of Wastwater (England's deepest Lake) is one of those peaks worth exploring, even though the scramble to the summit maybe a bit much for some, its stunning location is worth breaking the sweat. Coniston, Ullswater and Grasmere may attract tourists in their droves – due to the attraction of famous poets William Wordsworth (the museum is in Grasmere), and children's author 'Beatrix Potter', but they are iconic and a must for anyone visiting this part of the UK.

The Cumbrian Lake District is also home to some legendary hotels, so take time to enjoy the delicious flavours of locally produced cuisine. From teashops to Michelin Star restaurants, and pubs with real Cumberland ale, there is plenty of gastronomic delights.

Only an hour and a half from the Lake District is the sophisticated and stylish Manchester - the original 24-hour party city, home to famous super clubs. From fine dining and chic hotels to cutting-edge clubs and bars and the world's most progressive music scene, Manchester is buzzing – every night of the week.

The shopping here is legendary. With exclusive independent boutiques in the funky Northern Quarter, prestigious designer stores lining the Victorian, Neo-Gothic King Street and every conceivable type of market, you can shop to suit any budget. The Christmas markets (located throughout the city's squares) are the best in the UK. Stalls are set up for a month during November and December – selling produce from Germany, Austria, France which creates a lovely Christmas feel.

The past, the present and the future are intertwined in this city; historical landmarks complement bold, contemporary designs. World-class live events, international sporting competitions, and award-winning museums and galleries make Manchester one of the most entertaining places in the world. Add to this the passion of two premiership football clubs, and it's no wonder Manchester has become the 'capital of the north.'

Genre: Romantic Comedy
Destination: North West

Miss Potter (2006)

The name Beatrix Potter is synonymous with the English Lake District, and with Sawrey and Hawkshead in particular, for it was in this beautiful part of England that she wrote many of her children's books and here that she spent the last thirty years of her life, having married solicitor William Heelis in 1913. The film Miss Potter (played by Renee Zellweger) was shot in the Lake District, using all the famous outdoor scenes; interiors were shot in her private properties, which can still be visited today such as Yew Tree Farm, Beatrix Potter Gallery and Hill Top.

The film is an enchanting love story inspired by the life of Beatrix Potter, combining stories from her own life with animated sequences featuring characters from her stories, such as Peter Rabbit. When Beatrix finally settles in the Lake District, after her publisher and fiancé Norman Warne (played by Ewan McGregor) passes away she buys her farm house (Hill Top) and resumes her work in the comfort of her land and outbids other developers (with the help of Heelis) to preserve the nature – the land (which was donated after her death) and now forms part of the 'Lake district national park'. Who knows what would have happened to this pretty corner of the UK if it wasn't for Beatrix Potter's vision? It is without a doubt one of Britain's popular rural destinations.

Stylish Place to Stay

Yew Tree Farm, Coniston
Yew Tree Farm was owned by Beatrix potter in the 1930s and is still home to many of her furnishings, and of course was featured in the film 'Miss Potter'. It is primarily a farmhouse retreat, set in the Coniston countryside, with plenty of walks nearby such as 'Tarn Hows' and Coniston Old man. The historic tea room furnished by Beatrix Potter herself in 1930 is a gem, the fireside seating in winter and extra seating in the garden for sunny days.

Delicious Place to Eat

Sharrow Bay, Ullswater
Dining is 'fine' at Sharrow Bay, whether it be breakfast, lunch, dinner or the fabulous afternoon tea, is an experience like no other. Overlooking Lake Ullswater the Michelin star restaurant is an absolute gem. Its friendly, warm cosy atmosphere and stunning views is a special place for special occasions. Whilst their breakfast is a sure hit, their afternoon tea is the star of the show – served daily at both the Main house and Tudor style 'Bank House' the assortment of sweet fancies and carefully cut sandwiches washed down with copious amounts of champagne (or tea) is a real treat. Most importantly, Sharrow Bay was the original creator of Sticky Toffee Pudding. If there's a pudding to die for, this is it, as it was all those years ago and still as popular.

Genre: Romantic Comedy
Destination: North West

🎬 Looking for Eric (2009)

Seeing footballers at the Cannes film festival is becoming a bit of a tradition. So Eric Cantona's recent appearance is no surprise, the gnomic philosopher-king of 90s Man United, and now hero of Ken Loach's boisterous new picture; scripted by Paul Laverty, is a lovably good-natured if erratic comedy about a depressed middle-aged postman and football fan called Eric, played by Steve Evets. His chaotic family, his wild stepsons and the cement mixer in the front garden don't help, but it is Eric's own secret that drives him to the brink.

The film is set in Manchester and scenes are shot around the city centre and the football stadium 'Old Trafford'. So this film might not appeal to all (especially those who don't care for football or are avid Manchester City fans) but it's a quirky film that's shows a side of life we can all appreciate, and a side of Manchester not many have seen before.

🛏 Stylish Place to Stay

Great John Street, Manchester
Converted Victoria town house, which used to be the old school (a renowned hang-out for the staff at Granada Television) is now a sleek, hip boutique hotel situated in the centre of Manchester. A perfect location for exploring the city's highlights. The rooms have kept their traditional Victorian features, whilst being updated with roll-top baths and plasma TVs. It has the added bonus of a stunning roof terrace, where you can chill with a glass of wine while gazing out onto the cobbled streets of the famous soap opera 'Coronation Street'.

🍴 Delicious Place to Eat

Lounge Ten, Manchester
Whilst the eccentric owner will certainly make an impression on you – it's the décor and ambience that really sells this place. It's glamorous, sophisticated – yet homely at the same time. The lush furnishings, chez lounges, and chandeliers make this place feel exclusive – and it is. This place is a local celebrity hangout, and its easy to see why (there is a 'boudoir' private dining area). The food is modern British cuisine, yet they certainly don't skimp on the portion sizes.

Genre: Epics + Historical
Destination: Peak District

✦ Regional Information

Britain's first national park, the 'Peak District' established in 1951, lying mainly in northern Derbyshire, is an area of great diversity. With many lowlands, historic market towns and stunning stately homes its no wonder that it attracts an estimated 22 million visitors per year, and is thought to be the second most-visited national park in the world (after Mount Fuji National Park in Japan).

The landscapes of the Peak District have formed an inspiration to writers and have been popular settings for film and television. Key scenes in Jane Austen's 1813 novel Pride and Prejudice are set in the Derbyshire Peak District. Peveril of the Peak (1823) by Sir Walter Scott is a historical novel set at Peveril Castle, Castleton during the reign of Charles II. William Wordsworth was a frequent visitor to Matlock; the Peaks have inspired several of his poems, including an 1830 sonnet to Chatsworth House. The village of Morton in Charlotte Brontë's 1847 novel Jane Eyre is based on Hathersage, where Brontë stayed in 1845, and Thornfield Hall is said to have been inspired by nearby North Lees Hall.

In recent adaptations of Pride and Prejudice, Longnor has featured as Lambton, while Lyme Park and Chatsworth House have stood in for Pemberley. Haddon Hall not only doubled as Thornfield Hall in two different adaptations of Jane Eyre, but has also appeared in several other films including Elizabeth, The Princess Bride and The Other Boleyn Girl. Haddon Hall, situated two miles to the south of Bakewell on the A6, was mentioned in the Domesday Book and is perhaps the most perfect example of a medieval manor house in the country. The gardens are a delight and believed to be the most romantic in Britain, the colourful, walled garden falls in terraces towards the River Wye. 'The Duchess' was also recently filmed at 'Chatsworth House', which was recently named as Britains best stately home at the Best of British Awards.

Every year a number of prestigious events are held in the park, including the International Horse Trials in May and the Country Fair in August/September (a three day event from 2007). The house now remains open to visitors until just before Christmas. From early November the house takes on a magical appearance with fairy lights and candles and part of the garden floodlit. The shops and restaurants are transformed to offer the best seasonal food and gifts and the farmyard plays host to Father Christmas.

Buxton has a long history as a spa town (and famous for its mineral water) due to its geothermal spring and was initially developed by the Romans around AD 78, when the settlement was known as Aquae Arnemetiae, or the spa of the goddess of the grove. Today it is a very popular town due to its thriving art scene and notable buildings such as 'The Crescent' (1780–1784), modelled on Bath's Royal Crescent, 'The Devonshire' (1780–1789), 'The Natural Baths', and 'The Pump Room'.

Bakewell is a highly picturesque market town that crosses the River Wye and lies right in the heart of the Peak District National Park. Bakewell dates back to Saxon times and of course is home to the famous Bakewell pudding, which is a Peak District speciality (very different from the nationally available Bakewell tart), and the famous cheese Stilton, which area of production is the village of Hartington.

Above left. View of Bakewell. **Above right.**
The Original Bakewell Pudding Shop, both
images Courtesy of visitpeakdistrict.com.

Genre: Epics + Historical
Destination: Peak District

The Duchess

The movie explores the marriage, relationships, and passions of 18th century aristocrat Georgiana, Duchess of Devonshire, (played by Kiera Knightly). Georgiana Spencer became Duchess of Devonshire upon her marriage to the Duke (played by Ralph Fiennes) in 1774, at the height of the Georgian era, a period of fashion, decadence, and political change. Spirited and adored by the public at large she quickly found her marriage to be a disappointment, defined by her duty to produce a male heir and the Duke's philandering and callous indifference to her.

Keira Knightley is becoming renowned for her sumptuous and emotional period dramas, (she also starred in Pride & Prejudice) and alongside Ralph Fiennes they display credible and believable performances. The sets and locations also contribute to the films success – whilst filing took place at Twickenham Film Studios and on-location in Bath, Holkham Hall, Clandon Park, Kedleston Hall, Somerset House – it's the enchanting scenes at Chatsworth House that really inspires the audience. Chatsworth House is where Georgiana lived following her marriage to the Duke of Devonshire, and is one of Britain's best loved historic houses and estates, has been owned by the Duke and Duchess of Devonshire for over 450 years. The filming in the area has re-ignited tourism as many scenes were also shot in the Derbyshire countryside and Chatsworth House have added the wedding dresses worn by Keira Knightley, in the film's marriage scenes, to their collection of artifacts; which can still be visited today.

The cast and crew of 'The Duchess' sampled English charm while staying on the outskirts of Derby at the Breadsall Priory Hotel. Keira Knightley allegedly stayed at the Hurdlow Grange Cottage in the Peak District village of Longnor, which is available for holiday rentals.

Stylish Place to Stay

The Rutland Arms Hotel, Bakewell.
Set in the magnificent town of Bakewell in the heart of the Peak District this 19th century hotel offers elegance and distinct history amid unrivalled surroundings. It lies equal distance from both Matlock and Buxton, on the edge of the Chatsworth estate. The first ever Bakewell Pudding was made by a cook in the kitchens at the Rutland Arms. The timeless elegance of the hotel is marked by the 54 antique clocks which grace the public areas and portrayed in the 35 individually styled bedrooms, one of which it is believed that Jane Austin stayed in whist working on her novel Pride and Prejudice.

Delicious Place to Eat

Fischers at Baslow Hall, Bakewell.
Standing at the end of a winding chestnut-tree-lined driveway, on the edge of the Chatsworth Estate, (perfect after a day exploring the area) the house enjoys an enviable location surrounded by some of the country's finest stately homes, serving top end cuisine. Opt for the premium tasting menu (for £60.00) offering samples of different dishes and canapés to start.

Genre: Epics + Historical
Destination: Peak District

The Other Boleyn Girl

The Other Boleyn Girl is a historical fiction novel written by British author Philippa Gregory, based on the life of 16th-century aristocrat, adapted for screenplay. Mary Boleyn (played by Scarlett Johansson) and her sister Ann (played by Natalie Portman) are driven by their ambitious father and uncle to advance the family's power and status by courting the affections of the King of England (Eric Bana). Leaving behind the simplicity of country life, the girls are thrust into the dangerous and thrilling world of court life – and what began as a bid to help their family develops into a ruthless rivalry between Anne and Mary for the love of the king. Despite some criticism, over historical inaccuracies the novel (and film) has enjoyed high commercial success and it has a large and loyal fan-base in both Britain and America. Obviously the cast has helped propel the popularity of the film, but also the film locations which were used have fuelled interest in British history and culture. Several National Trust properties were brought back to life during the filming, such as Great Chalfield Manor (based in Wiltshire) which was altered to become an accurate portrayal of the Boleyn country home

and Knole in Sevenoaks which was used for the internal courtyard and deer park scenes.

The film was also partly set in the Derbyshire Peak District with scenes shot in and around North Lees Hall at Hathersage, Haddon Hall, Cavedale, and Dovedale.

Stylish Place to Stay

North Lees Hall, Hathersage
North Lees Hall was built circa in 1590 by the famous Elizabethan architect, Robert Smythson who was responsible for Hardwick Hall. William Jessop and his family of twelve children were the first inhabitants of North Lees Hall although the building's most celebrated tenants were the Eyre family. This is a 17th century 'tower house,' in an amazing location in the Peaks District. The main bedroom includes a canopied bed straight out of the Elizabethan era. Persian rugs were scattered in each room. Very well equipped and functional kitchen with rooftop patio with panoramic view of the surrounding area. Perfect for a week long stay in the area.

Delicious Place to Eat

The Walnut Club, Hathersage
Their head chef Nicholas Wilson has previously worked with the well respected Jean Christophe Novelli and they make no pretence about their own aim to achieve Michelin star recognition. The place has quite a lively feel at weekend with Jazz bands playing throughout the evenings. It is becoming the place to be seen; serving 100% organic award winning food to a host of celebrity visitors such as Paul Newman, Michael Vaughan, Lynn Faulds-Wood and Clarissa Dickson Wright of Two Fat Ladies fame. So make sure you dress to impress...

THE TRAVEL
BOOKSHOP

Focus On...
London

London is a world renowned city for many reasons, being home to the British monarchy and the centre for famous musicals. Movie directors have long used London as a film backdrop, such as romantic comedies like Bridget Jones' Diary, Notting Hill and period dramas like Shakespeare in Love and The Queen.

The 1999 hit movie 'Notting Hill' staring Julia Roberts as Anna Scott, the most famous woman in the world, and Hugh Grant as William Thacker, the owner of a local bookshop (pictured left), helped put this area on the map. Thacker's dream comes true as actress Anna Scott appears in his humble bookshop and against the odds love blossoms. The film involves many locations around central London, in addition to Notting Hill; Anna and William can be seen at the Nobu Restaurant in the up-market area of Mayfair and are seen at the end of the film attending the premiere of her movie at the UCI Empire cinema in Leicester Square.

Notting Hill is a popular area and well known locally prior to this film due to the annual Notting Hill Carnival. It attracts one million participants every year, although the early history of the carnival was sometimes troubled, but with the support of public figures such as Prince Charles, there was a change in the policing of the event and it was no longer directed at stopping it but instead at helping it to pass safely, this has helped to transform the carnival into an international tourist attraction.

Many historic sites across the UK were used for Shakespeare in Love, but in London various locations including the Middle Temple Great Hall, Spitalfields, Barts Hospital and Marble Hill Palace were used. The film tells a largely fictitious story, but does use characters from real life and also makes allusions to various Shakespeare plays. The story focuses on William Shakespeare's (played by Joseph Fiennes) forbidden love for Viola de Lesseps (Gwyneth Paltrow).

Obviously one of the best times of year to visit London is the summer (July or August) when there are plenty of summer festivals and long daylight days where you can relax in one of the many pretty parks (weather permitting of course!). The best way to get around London and to visit all the famous sights is by bike or open bus. 'GoPedal' drop off and collect bikes to any location – they also provide helpful cycle maps where you can definitely cycle the heart of London in a day taking in the impressive sights such as Regents Park, Tower Bridge and Buckingham Palace. Many of London's museums also offer free entry while historic or cultural attractions like the Tower of London, and the Shakespeare Globe Theatre charge an entry fee.

There are also plenty of walks around the city. 'Secret London Walks' will lead you in the footsteps of Jude Law, Hugh Grant, Ralph Fiennes, Renée Zellweger and other stars of the big screen to discover some of London's famous film locations.

General Information

Tourist Information
www.visitbritain.co.uk

Eurostar
www.eurostar.com
T. +44 (0) 8705 186 186
(Booking line)

Virgin Trains
www.virgintrains.co.uk
T. +44 (0) 8457 222 333
(Booking line)

Orient Express Trains
www.orient-express.com
T. +44 (0) 845 077 2222
(Booking line)
E. oereservations.uk@orient-express.com

Scotland & Northumberland

General Tourist Information

Visit Fort William
www.visit-fortwilliam.co.uk

The Royal Scotsman
www.royalscotsman.com
T. +44 (0)845 077 2222

Edinburgh Fringe festival
www.edfringe.com
T. +44 (0)131 226 0026
E. admin@edfringe.com

Glengoyne Whisky Distillery
www.glengoyne.com
T.+44 (0)1360 550 254
E. reception@glengoyne.com

Edinburgh Hogmanay
www.edinburghshogmanay.org

Wallace Monument Information
www.nationalwallacemonument.com
T. +44 (0) 1786 472140
E. info@nationalwallacemonument.com

Lothian Helicopters
Braveheart Forth Valley Tour
www.lothianhelicopters.co.uk
T. +44 (0)1875 320032
E. info@lothianhelicopters.co.uk

West Coast Railways
Jacobite Steam Railway Tour
www.steamtrain.info
T. +44 (0)845 415 3131
(Booking line)

Hadrians Wall Information
www.nationaltrail.co.uk/hadrianswall

Durham Cathedral
www.durhamcathedral.co.uk
T. +44 (0) 191 386 4266

Alnwick Castle
www.alnwickcastle.com
T. +44 (0) 1665 510777

The Winnock Hotel
www.winnockhotel.com
T. +44 (0) 1360 660245
E. info@winnockhotel.com

Langley Castle
www.langleycastle.com
T. +44 (0) 1434 688 888
E. manager@langleycastle.com

Lilburns
Paikes Street, Alnwick, between the
Market Place & Bondgate
T. +44(0)1665 603444
Open: 10.00–22.00 Mon-Sat

The Clachan Inn
2 Main Street, Drymen, G63 0BG
T. +44 (0) 845 8334169

North West

Lake District National Park
Tourist Information
www.lake-district.gov.uk

Lake District
General Information
www.golakes.co.uk

Manchester Tourist information
www.visitmanchester.com

Manchester United FC Tours
www.manutd.com
T. +44 (0)161 868 8000
E. tours@manutd.co.uk

Luxury Lake Cruises
www.lakedistrictboatcharter.co.uk
T. +44 (0)7717 207 583
E. info@lakedistrictboatcharter.co.uk

Official tour guides of Manchester
www.toursofmanchester.co.uk
T. +44 (0)161 864 2640

The Beatrix Potter Properties
www.beatrixpottersociety.org.uk

Miss Potter Film Tours
www.misspotter-tours.co.uk
T. +44 (0) 17687 75337

Yew Tree Farm
www.yewtree-farm.com
T. +44 (0) 15394 41433
E. info@yewtree-farm.co.uk

Sharrow Bay
www.sharrowbay.co.uk
T. +44 (0) 1768 486301
E. info@sharrowbay.co.uk

Great John Street
www.greatjohnstreet.co.uk
T. +44 (0) 161 831 3210
E. info@greatjohnstreet.co.uk

Lounge Ten
www.lounge10manchester.co.uk
T. +44 (0) 161 834 1331
E. lounge10@btconnect.com
Open: 12.00–14.30, 21.00–23.00
Mon-Fri

Peak District

Peak District Tourist Information
www.peakdistrict.org

Official Tourist Board Information
www.visitpeakdistrict.com

The Bakewell Tart shop
www.bakewelltartshop.co.uk
T. +44 (0)1629 814692

Haddon Hall
www.haddonhall.co.uk
T. +44 (0)1629 812855
E. info@haddonhall.co.uk

Chatsworth House
www.chatsworthhouse.org
T. +44 (0)1246 565300
Open: House 11.00–17.30, Gardens
11.00–18.00

North Lees Hall
www.vivat.org.uk
T. +44 (0) 207 336 8825

Rutland Arms
www.rutlandarmsbakewell.co.uk
T. +44 (0) 1629812812
E. enquiries@rutlandbakewell.co.uk

The Walnut Club
www.thewalnutclub.com
T. +44 (0) 1433 651155
Open: Tues, Weds, Thurs & Sun
12.00–19.00, Fri & Sat 12.00–
23.30

Fischers
www.fischers-baslowhall.co.uk
T. +44 (0) 1246 583 259

London

Buckingham Palace VIP Tours
www.royalcollection.org.uk
T. +44 (0)20 7766 7300

Go Pedal
Bike ride around London
www.gopedal.co.uk
T. +44 (0) 7850 796320
E. info@gopedal.co.uk

Secret London Walks and Visits
www.secretlondonwalks.co.uk
T. +44 (0) 20 8881 2933
E. diane@secretlondonwalks.co.uk

The Travel Bookshop
www.thetravelbookshop.com
T. +44 (0)20 7229 5260
E. post@thetravelbookshop.com

Notting Hill Carnival
www.thenottinghillcarnival.com

Nobu Restaurant
Old Park Lane
www.noburestaurants.com
T. +44 (0)20 7447 4747

The Punch Bowl, Mayfair
www.punchbowllondon.com
T. +44 (0)20 7493 6841
E. info@punchbowllondon.com

The Ritz, Piccadilly
www.theritzlondon.com
T. +44 (0)20 7493 8181
E. enquire@theritzlondon.com

SPAIN

Catalonia | West Andalucia |
East Andalucia | Madrid

🏆 Why is this place so special?

Spain is the third most popular tourist country in the world, and it's not hard to see why. Every one of the 17 regions has its own characteristics and is still very much influenced by the different cultures, languages and geographies of the separate kingdoms that once ruled them, which, in addition to all that sun, sea, sand, and sangria explains why it is such a fascinating destination. Not to mention the string of annual traditional festivals and fiestas throughout the year such as the bull running of Pamplona and the fireworks of Las Fallas, which generally revolve around Catholic saints and historical events, which now have somewhat of a cult following.

Some of the best tourist attractions can be found in Barcelona, the Capital of Catalonia (Northeast) and second largest city, which has been the home of many famous artists of Spain; such as splendid architecture by Gaudi, and painters such as Dali and Picasso who spent long periods in Catalonia. This city has been used as a movie backdrop due to the Gothic architecture and winding back streets for a variety of both independent films as well as Hollywood blockbusters. Of course it's not just Barcelona that has become popular for filmmakers. Andalucia has also been known to crop up several times in films.

The Tabernas Desert in Andalucia is famous for being the film location for many Westerns, featuring stars like Clint Eastwood and epics such as 'Lawrence of Arabia' - with its vast area is Europe's only semi-desert and its canyons and rocky landscape makes it an intriguing place to visit. Beyond the touristic beaches of Andalucias' 'Costa del Sol' that line the coastal areas, are the famous 'white villages' (Pueblos Blancos) that scatter the area. The region also attracts history buffs due to the stunning and impressive Alhambra Palace and Fortress and of course the beautiful city of Seville, which boasts a majestic cathedral and is the proud home of flamenco. Not to mention the

Plaza de España which was used as a backdrop for
Lucas' film 'Star Wars II: attack of the clones.'
In the centre of Spain lies Madrid, the capital
since 1576 and host to many historical Spanish
monuments. The Royal castle and Spanish
museums like el Prado and Reina Sofia (with
paintings of Velasquez, Goya, Miro and Picasso)
are only a few of the many great Spanish tourist
attractions the city represents, but its football,
shopping and nightlife have become renowned for
overseas visitors. Madrid also hit the movie world
as a famous backdrop for David Lean's film Doctor
Zhivago (1965), as it was impossible to do location
shooting in Moscow at the time.

Spain is no longer a destination for the
stereotype package holidays it was once deemed
in the 1980s. It has become so accessible from
the UK, (mainly due to the low cost airlines) that it
has become popular for couples wanting a quick
escape for a weekend, to intrepid travellers using
it as a gateway for a longer trip to North Africa.

📖 Fast Facts

Capital: Madrid.

Location: Western Europe, surrounded by
the Mediterranean Sea. Frontiers with
Portugal, Andorra and France.

Population: 47 million.

Religion: Protestant Roman Catholic.

Languages: Spanish 100%, Catalan, Galician
and Basque also spoken regionally.

✈ Getting there and exploring around

Spain is dotted with international airports and its connections with the rest of Europe are excellent. You can of course reach Spain by ferry and train from the UK if you don't want to fly and if you have lots of time to spare. Most of Spain is well covered by both bus and rail networks. On the other hand, if your trip to Spain is part of a wider European tour, then it may be worth investing in a rail pass, such as the InterRail ticket.

Buses tend to be quicker than trains and will also normally take you closer to your destination. The majority of train stations are several kilometres from the city they serve and you've no guarantee of a connecting bus.

Hiring a car in Spain will never be your cheapest option, but it might be the most convenient. If you want to explore some of the Spain's harder-to-reach regions, like Alpujarras, the Rías Bajas (to the west of Santiago de Compostela) or the region around Cadiz and Tarifa, renting a car is your best choice. Taxis are a good way to get around all Spain cities, but can get pretty expensive.

In the major cities (such as Madrid, Barcelona) there are open top tourist buses which can take your around the major sights, which is a good idea if it's the height of summer. There are also plenty of 'walking tour' companies who can also show you the cities highlights.

☼ Best time of year to visit

July and August are the busiest periods for international travellers, so if you want to go somewhere where you won't hear too much English, the Costa Brava at this time of year is not the place to be. As summer is unbearably hot especially in internal cities like Madrid and Seville, as the Spanish themselves evacuate these cities and escape to the cooler coast. The best time for city sightseeing is undoubtedly spring (April/May) and autumn (September/October).

However, it can be tempting to visit Spain at the hottest time of year to guarantee some sunshine, and of course some of the festivals. Although Spain has a number of local festivals throughout the year, such as Las Fallas in Valencia (in March) and La Tomatina in Valencia (the tomato throwing festival) happening in late August as well as the Pamplona, San fermin festival (running of the bulls) held in July.

Seville is the place to be for Semana Santa (Easter) and the Feria de Sevilla (a festival of bullfighting and flamenco) occurring in April. Semana Santa is a popular time to travel for the Spanish themselves, as is the week between Christmas and New Year. So you might find it difficult to get accommodation during these times, so book in advance.

February is also carnival month, with the biggest events appearing in Cadiz and the Canary Islands. Plenty is also going on in Catalonia during September, with the Festa de Santa Tecla in Tarragona and the Festa de Mercé in Barcelona. In October, catch the Bienal de Flamenco, Spain's biggest flamenco festival, every two years (2008, 2010) as well as a whole host of film festivals.

? Must know before you go

Getting caught out. Public toilets are rare in Spain so the best places are department stores or bars and restaurants where you are a customer.

Nightlife hours. Nightlife in Spain is in a class of its own, particularly from Thursday to Sunday. Pubs, late night haunts (bares de copas) and discotheques normally keep open until 3 or 4 in the morning, and in the major cities, such as Madrid and Barcelona, there are innumerable night-spots that stay open till dawn.

Tapas for tea. There are many little bars and old taverns where you can go to have a beer and some 'tapas' (small pieces of food that go along with the drink) just before lunch (as an appetizer) or even instead of lunch if you have a few!

Highlights

Bright lights of Barcelona. Numerous attractions such as the Sagrada Familia (Gaudi), the Gothic Cathedral, the lively Ramblas, the Gothic Quarter, La Barceloneta (Old Port), Park Güell, Teatro Liceum, and the 100 year amusement park Tibidabo.

Sights of Seville. Home of the Europe´s biggest Cathedral and its adjacent minaret, La Giralda. Among the many sights of the city are the Torre del Oro, the atmospheric Barrio Santa Cruz 'Old Jewish Quarter', Reales Alcazares and gardens, Plaza de Toros and the magnificent Plaza de Espana situated by the Maria Luisa Park.

Alhambra in Granada. Explore the wonderful Islamic architecture at the Alhambra palace and fortress at the southeastern border of Granada.

Madness in Madrid. Spend a night at one of the many late nightclubs and end the evening with chocolate con churros (thick hot chocolate with deep-fried hoops of batter). Just what you need after a night on the tiles!

★ Star Spotting

Preferred choice of top models and temperamental rock stars (P. Diddy reportedly partied up a storm here when he came to Barcelona to host the 2002 MTV Awards) is the Hotel Arts, on the Marina has remained a jet-set playground and symbol of 'cool Barcelona' for over a decade.

Genre: Romantic Comedy
Destination: Catalonia

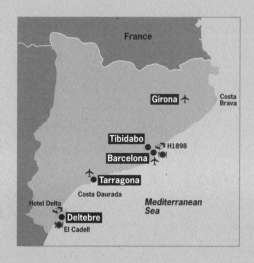

✈ Regional Information

Catalonia is perhaps best known for its vibrant capital, Barcelona, and of course the Mediterranean coastline 'Costa Brava', with ample beaches and mild climate, doubtlessly a first rate touristic attraction. Around the 1950s Hollywood studios were drawn to the area and several high profile movies were filmed there, as it was much to do with cheap filming costs as well as the scenery. Nevertheless the Costa Brava was presented to the world. However Catalonia also offers high mountain ranges, the Pyrenees in the north, the curious formations of Montserrat, the inactive volcanoes of Garrotxa, and a wide plain area in the region's centre. In addition the peaks of the Pyrenees mountain range offer excellent skiing opportunity in the shape of Andorra, & nearby Barcelona is one of the world's most popular city break destinations.

Barcelona, Spain is without doubt one of Europe's most exciting cities. Barcelona is a place of extraordinary architectural dazzle, achieved by what has been called both Catalan Art Nouveau and Modernism, by architects such as Gaudi. Monumental sculptures by local masters like Joan Miró adorn public spaces and museums house extraordinary treasures ranging from works of the ancient Romans to those of Pablo Picasso and Salvador Dalí. Barcelona city is further enhanced by brightly coloured outdoor markets, the lively shopping area of 'Las Rambla' a magnificent Mediterranean port where yachts sway peacefully, and a plentiful array of stylish seafood restaurants. Needless to say, the nightlife is splendid. The city also has a fabulous viewpoint from mountain 'Tibidabo' at 512 meters it is the tallest mountain in the Serra de Collserola, which is not to be missed. Rising sharply to the north-west, it affords spectacular views over the city and the surrounding coastline. There is a 100 year old amusement park, a telecommunications tower (Torre de Collserola), and a Catholic church, the Temple de Sagrat Cor, at the top, all of which are visible from most of the city. Designed by Enric Sagnier, the church took 60 years to construct and is topped by a sculpture of the Sacred Heart by Josep Miret Llopart. The Amusement park is the oldest in Barcelona and retains most of the original rides, some of which date to the turn of the 20th century. Tibidabo can be reached by a funicular (built in 1901) and by the traditional and charming 'blue tram'.

Tarragona is the southernmost province in Catalonia, Spain, which also boasts a capital of the same name. Located on the Costa Dorada, Tarragona and its beautiful beaches are perfect for basking in the sun. But Tarragona is also home to ancient vestiges standing testament to Spain's glorious past; the diverse archaeological complexes and museums spread about the Tarragona province and its capital are perfect for you. Just walk around towns like the picturesque Reus or the hectic Salou and discover its important heritage, along with the lifestyle of its hospitable dwellers. Also nature lovers are welcome, since the chances offered by Tarragona's natural parks and gardens are immense.

Being situated in the north east corner of Spain; bordering France, Andorra and the Mediterranean, Catalonia enjoys a privileged location. Outdoor lovers can enjoy a wide range of activities such as skiing, hiking, mountains biking and sunbathing, thanks to a varied relief which endows Catalonia with clearly differentiated landscapes. Temperatures depend on the area, severe on the interior and milder on the coast. Catalonia also has a very marked culture of its own, most evidently of Mediterranean tradition, and is distinguished of most other Spanish regions in several aspects, not at least by its language, Catalonian (although everybody speaks and understands Castilian Spanish perfectly).

In Catalonia good eating is a matter of priority for most. Catalonian cuisine, which has been subject to so many influences, is sophisticated, flavoursome and varied. Fish and seafood are always fresh, and sausages and meats are of the best quality. This cuisine features delectable cold dishes like exqueixada (desalted cod salad), escalivada (roast aubergines, onions and red peppers) and xató (curly endive lettuce, cod and anchovies). Most popular dishes in Catalan gastronomy are butifarra (Catalan sausage with beans), longaniza (local spiced sausage) and fuet (a delicious type of salami). In addition, Catalonia is one of Spain's great wine-growing regions and where its most popular beverage is the champagne-like cava (sparkling wine).

The other major attractions which make this region so special are the historic city of Girona and its old Jewish quarter, Figueres which was the birthplace of painter Salvador Dali, the golden coastline of Costa Dorada, stretching from south to Tarragona (which was an important city of the Roman empire and still preserves outstanding monuments such as Tomb of the Scorpios) and finally Lerida home of the cathedral 'Seo' located inland a mountainous area.

Genre: Romantic Comedy
Destination: Catalonia

Vicky Cristina Barcelona (2008)

A quirky, sassy, Woody Allen film set in stunning Barcelona. The plot centers on two American women, Vicky (Rebecca Hall) and Cristina (Scarlett Johansson) who decide to spend a summer in Barcelona, where they meet an artist (played by Javier Bardem) who is attracted to both of them while still enamoured of his mentally and emotionally unstable ex-wife María Elena (played by Penélope Cruz). The film was shot in Avilés, Barcelona, and Oviedo, and was Allen's fourth consecutive film shot outside of the United States and won the Golden Globe Award for Best Motion Picture – Musical or Comedy. In 2007, controversy arose in Catalonia because the film (allegedly) was partially funded with public money: Barcelona's city hall provided one million. Either way there is no doubt the film showcases some of the city's highlights such as the picturesque mountain 'Tibidabo' where they shot several scenes at the 100 year old amusement park. The film also portrays many typical cultural delights of Catalonia such as the Spanish guitar sessions and drinking and dining 'al fresco', and the Gaudi art scene which can be experienced by many on a visit to Barcelona or the region.

Stylish Place to Stay

H1898, Barcelona

Stunning, elegant and colonial hotel located on La Rambla. It has a very contemporary interior with spacious rooms and best of all, a magnificent rooftop terrace with a dip pool overlooking some of the city's landmark buildings. Probably one of the best features is the 'cave' like spa area which is a real sanctuary from the hustle and bustle above, which offer 'spice' inspired treatments. The hotel is aptly named after the year in which the final Spanish colonies, the Philippines and Cuba, gained independence. The building was once the headquarters for the Filipino Tobacco Company.

Delicious Place to Eat

Restaurant En Ville, Barcelona

Tucked away down the back streets behind La Ramla, is this local rustic, eatery with intimate live Spanish guitar sessions Thursday, Fridays and Saturday evenings. The food is a delightful mixture of Catalan and Spanish cuisine, with its piece de resistance being the 'Patatas Bravas' and plate of local meats. The deserts are also to die for.

Genre: Romantic Comedy
Destination: Catalonia

Sahara (2005)

Sahara (starring Penelope Cruz and Matthew McConaughy) maybe more of an action adventure plot than a romantic comedy, but there are elements of comedy and a romantic build up between this pair, to warrant a new genre. The film was based on the best-selling novel by Clive Cussler, and opened at the US box office grossing $18 million on its first weekend.

The plot features around Master explorer and former US Navy Seal Dirk Pitt (McConaughy) and his wisecracking buddy Al Giordino goes on the adventure of a lifetime of seeking out a lost Civil War ironclad battleship known as the 'Ship of Death' that protects a secret cargo is lost somewhere in the deserts of West Africa. But while the two cross paths with a beautiful and brilliant U.N. scientist Dr. Eva Rojas (Cruz) who is being hounded by a ruthless dictator. She believes that the hidden treasure may be connected to a larger problem that threatens the world around them. Hunting for a ship that no one else thinks exists, Dirk, Al, and Eva must rely on their wits and their daring heroics to outsmart dangerous warlords, survive the threatening terrain, and get to the bottom of both mysteries.

It may have been set in Morocco, and most of the desert locations were filmed near Erfoud, a tiny town on the edge of the Sahara, near the Algerian border, but several scenes were filmed in Cruz' native Spain. While in Spain, the crew shot several scenes in Barcelona, which doubled for Lagos, Nigeria; the city's Natural History Museum received a major dress to play the part of a Nigerian museum. "We had 150 extras in native costume," says Cameron. "We dressed the entire room with Nigerian and Tuareg artefacts. The amazing thing about this building is that it doesn't feel Spanish at all; we felt it looked like a Lagos building. It has that feel to it." The planes of 'Delta del Ebro' in Tarragona province were also used for filming some of the scenes, which is the second largest wetland area in the western Mediterranean, after the French Camargue.

Stylish Place to Stay

Hotel Delta, Deltebre

Built in old deltaic style, Delta Hotel is a family-run property surrounded by gardens and situated in Deltebre. It's a perfect location for exploring the stunning local scenery by horseback, bike or by foot. It is also 83 kms from Universal's Port Aventura Theme Park (which offers a choice of hair-raising rollercoasters and live shows). The hotel has very basic but have comfortable rooms and a pretty swimming pool.

Delicious Place to Eat

El Cadell, Deltebre

El Cadell located in the Capital City of the Delta del Ebro, where Jesus y Maria and La cava which melt together to form just one town: Deltebre. Is an excellent restaurant to taste fresh fish of the day and an El Xapadillo (which is a local dried eel with salt and red pepper) served with Delta rice. The Port is situated on the left side of the river.

Genre: Science Fiction
Destination: West Andalucia

Regional Information

Andalucia, is known to many as 'the bridge between two continents' or 'the gateway to Europe' as it's where Africa meets Europe, both geographically and culturally, and is still the most 'typically Spanish' region of Spain. Perhaps the most unique feature is the remnants of its Moorish past. The Moors were a mixture of Berbers and Arabs who crossed into Spain from North Africa in 711 and within a mere four years they virtually conquered the whole of the Iberian Peninsula. Under the Muslims, the name Al-Andalus was applied to a much larger area than the present Spanish region, and at some periods it referred to nearly the entire Iberian Peninsula; it survived, however, as the name of the area where Muslim rule and culture persisted the longest, and remnants of its ruling past can still be witnessed today throughout its culture, music and gastronomy.

The diversity of the landscapes, which form the Andalusia region, provides an entire spectrum, and it is this variety of environments that create a superb mix of tourist attractions, which range from the monumental towns to traditional whitewash villages (called 'pueblos blancos'). Andalucia, is perhaps responsible for Spain's most enduring stereotypes - gypsy passion, bullfighting, flamenco, and extravagant Catholicism - it is also a continual source of inspiration for all types of artists (such as Spanish film director Carlos Saura who evokes the vibe of Andalucia in his films).

Andalucia is made up of the eight provinces of Huelva, Seville, Cádiz, Cordoba, Málaga, Jaén, Granada and Almería each known for its own special character. The west side of Andalusia which covers Seville, Cadiz and Huelva, is famed for bullfighting, colonial architecture, and cured jamon (ham) respectively.

Seville is perhaps best known for its bullfighting, Semana Santa (Easter festival) and striking monuments such as the Alcazar and the Giralda tower. The area is also fairly green with 'get-away-from-it-all style retreats' scattered around the nearby countryside and the Sierra del Norte Natural Park, which is great place for rock climbing or hiking enthusiasts. The city is now third in popularity - behind Barcelona and

Madrid - as a destination for city breaks partly because of the influx of low-cost airlines which now fly directly from the UK.

Cádiz province boasts beautiful coastline, nature reserves and the famous Pueblos Blancos. Here, the coastline is much better-preserved than the nearby Costa del Sol and it's not only perfect for sunbathing but also bird watching (such as the Bahía de Cádiz Natural Park) and scuba diving (along the straits of Gibraltar). What's more the town of Tarifa is famed for windsurfing as the Atlantic winds create ideal conditions
and kite surfing is also growing in popularity here. There are even more nature reserves inland most notably the Sierra de Grazelma National Park a small section of the Doñana National Park, which Cádiz shares with Huelva and Seville. You'll find a privileged biodiversity here, including vultures and eagles, and this great hiking territory is renowned for its rugged limestone landscape.

Finally Huelva, famous for quality cured meats such as jamón de Jabugo (cured ham) from (considered by some the best in Spain), is one of the least visited regions in Andalucia, it has a long Atlantic coastline with miles of unspoilt and often uncrowded beaches and forms part of the evocatively named Costa de la Luz (Coast of Light) that continues into Cadiz province. This coastline is rich in maritime history; most famously, it is where Christopher Columbus found his crew and ships and set sail for the New World.

Due to the diverse scenery (deserts to beaches), real Spanish culture, old villages and fairly consistent warm weather the region has become a bit of a favourite with film directors such as Lucas, Spielberg, Lean, Zefirelli or Almodóvar. Films ranging from Lawrence of Arabia to the Indiana Jones or James Bond series; have all been filmed in the region.

Genre: Science Fiction
Destination: West Andalucia

Star Wars II: Attack of the Clones (2002)

Star Wars Episode II: Attack of the Clones is the fifth Star Wars film, and the second part of the prequel trilogy which began with The Phantom Menace and ended with Revenge of the Sith. The film is set ten years after the Battle of Naboo, when the galaxy is on the brink of civil war. When an assassination attempt is made on Senator Padmé Amidala, the former Queen of Naboo (Natalie Portman), Jedi apprentice Anakin Skywalker (Hayden Christensen) is assigned to protect her, while his mentor Obi-Wan Kenobi is assigned to investigate the assassination attempt. Soon the Jedi are drawn into the heart of the separatist movement, and the beginning of a new threat to the galaxy: the Clone Wars. The film was a financial success, grossing over $300 million at the box office in United States and filmed in seductive locations, Italy, Spain and Tunisia. Exterior shots of Naboo (which was entirely computer-generated in The Phantom Menace) is the Palaçio Español, a semi-circular arcaded building in Seville, built for the 1929 Spanish-American exhibition. In the Plaza itself you'll find the canal, crossed by elegant 'Venetian' bridges over which Anakin and Padme walk with R2-D2. The colonnades of the plaza were also used as a hotel in Cairo from the classic film 'Lawrence of Arabia'.

Stylish Place to Stay

Hacienda San Rafael, Seville
Set in a 350 acre farm this old olive farm is only a stones throw away from bustling Seville. It has been beautifully restored in the traditional colonial Andalucian style and has managed to retain many of its original features. Large, well furnished rooms set around the patio and elegant public areas, such as the beautiful sitting rooms all add up to a great, informal atmosphere. Then there are the three enchanting 'casitas' (thatched houses) with their own private garden and infinity pool.

Delicious Place to Eat

El Rinconcillo, Seville
El Rinconcillo is something of a victim of its enduring reputation, because, as the oldest of all Seville tapas bars, it was always going to attract its fair share of visitors. More often than not, tourists tend to have a quick drink and a glance around at the lovely traditional tiles and head straight off again. Stay, and your reward is a selection of the best value tapas around (mini portions of arroz come particularly recommended…) washed down with a glass or two of ice-cold fino.

Genre: Science Fiction
Destination: West Andalucia

Die Another Day

Die Another Day (2002) is the twentieth spy film in the James Bond series, and the fourth and last to star Pierce Brosnan as the MI6 agent James Bond. In the pre-title sequence, Bond leads a mission to North Korea, during which he is found out and, after killing a rogue North Korean colonel, he is captured and imprisoned. As with many of the Bond films, the producers never seem to scrimp on using exotic film locations to depict everything from love scenes to car chases. This film is no exception. The film was shot primarily in the United Kingdom, Iceland, and Cádiz, Spain. Other locations included Pinewood Studios' historic 007 Stage, and scenes shot in Maui, Hawaii, in December 2001. Laird Hamilton and other professional surfers were hired to perform in the pre-title surfing scene, which was shot near Cádiz and Newquay, Cornwall. Scenes inside Graves' diamond mine were also filmed in Cornwall, at the Eden Project. The scenes featuring Berry in a bikini were shot in Cádiz; the location was reportedly cold and windy, and footage has been released of Berry wrapped in thick towels between takes to avoid catching a chill. The scenes involving the Cuban locations Havana and the fictional Isla Los Organos were filmed at La Caleta, Spain. Cadiz, also stood in for the Cuban capital, but the interior of the cigar factory, where Bond drops the magic name Universal Exports in his search for Zao, is Simpson House, north London.

Stylish Place to Stay

V Boutique Hotel, Near Cadiz
This is a James Bond lair with stunning views of the surrounding countryside and windswept beaches – as well as the Moroccan skyline looking across the water. The 17th-century mansion with a tajine-style Moorish feel has only 12 rooms, which makes it an ideal intimate place to escape back to after days of sunbathing and kite-surfing on the nearby Costa de la Luz.

Delicious Place to Eat

El Faro, Cadiz
Gonzalo Cordoba's reputed favourite restaurant located in the fishing quarter, which justly deserves its reputation as being the top restaurant in the province. On the outside it's low key, with one of many low white houses decorated with bright blue flowerpots, but once inside, the decor is cosy with tiled walls, oil paintings and black and white photos of old Cadiz. Hams hang from the ceiling of the bar and the counter is piled high with oranges.

Seafood dominates the menu, but there are plenty of alternatives, such as venison in blue cheese sauce.

Genre: Action + Adventure
Destination: East Andalucia

Restaurante Las Tomasas
Alhambra Palace
Granada • Hotel Alhambra Palace
Sierra Nevada
Caboneras
La Joya de Cabo de Gata
Bitacora
Almeria •
San José

Mediterranean Sea

✦ Regional Information

Andalusian culture is deeply influenced by more than seven centuries of Muslim rule, which lasted from the Middle Ages until the Renaissance. Córdoba became the largest and richest city in Western Europe and the Moors established universities in Andalucia.

Perhaps the most unique features of this enchanting region are the remnants of this Moorish past. The Moors were a mixture of Berbers and Arabs who crossed into Spain from North Africa in 711 and within a mere four years they virtually conquered the whole of the Iberian Peninsula. Each of the Andalusian capitals boasts spectacular remains of Moorish monuments, the most unforgettable of which is, undoubtedly, Granada's mesmerising Alhambra palace.

The Alhambra, is a UNESCO world heritage site, literally meaning 'the red one' is a palace and fortress complex occupying a hilly terrace on the southeastern border of the city of Granada. Once the residence of the Muslim rulers of Granada and their court, the Alhambra is now one of Spain's major tourist attractions (and a renowned filming set for Indiana Jones) exhibiting the country's most famous Islamic architecture, together with Christian 16th century and later interventions in buildings and gardens that marked its image as it can be seen today.

The city of Granada itself was once the capital of the Caliphate of Granada and its magnificent Alhambra Palace is a testament to its importance. Today it's a charming town with winding streets that smell both of history and the allegedly best tapas in Spain. One of the most amazing things about the Granada Province is the mountains (known as the Sierra Nevada region) which are only about an hour's drive from the coast, so one moment you can be hiking amongst snow-tipped peaks and the next you can be bathing in under the blazing sun on the beach.

Almeria, located eastern of Granada, was one of the most important ports of Caliphate of Cordoba and the grandeur of its cathedral and the sumptuous Moorish Alcazaba citadel framed by narrow streets and whitewashed houses of the historic quarter are a poignant testimony to its distant Arabic origins. Apart from some great beaches, in the area, Almeria province is best-known for its desert landscape and climate which made it an ideal setting for Western films of the 1960s.

The Tabernas desert which lies to the north of the town of Almería between the mountains of Los Filabres and Alhamilla and is approximately 45 minutes drive from Garrucha, has a very similar landscape to North Africa. Making it also popular film location for westerns and action movies such as Indiana Jones, King of Kings, The Good the Bad and the Ugly, Conan and the Peter O'Toole classic, Lawrence of Arabia, a Fistful of Dollars and much later 800 Bullets. The making of these films and stars like Clint Eastwood, Raquel Welch, Peter O'Toole and Charles Bronson, to name but a few, gave rise to the name of 'Mini Hollywood', this name is still used today to refer to this arid area. There are a few 'adventure' companies springing up that offer desert experiences and trekking – but perhaps one of the best ways to explore the desert is by horseback.

If you are looking for peaceful coves and sand dunes, unspoilt beaches, imposing mountain cliffs, charming villages and deep waters ideal for swimming or diving, you should head for the Cabo de Gata-Níjar Natural Park between San José and Carboneras on the eastern coast

Genre: Action + Adventure
Destination: East Andalucia

Indiana Jones and the Last Crusade (1989)

Harrison Ford is synonymous with his character and archaeologist adventurer Indiana Jones. And for anyone who grew up in the 1980s, 'Indy' was the coolest man in history. Part of the success of the films was down to the action scenes, but the spectacular locations where his adventures took place were all part of the magic formula. Indiana Jones and the Last Crusade was the third film in the series, which as supposed to be his last, but was followed at a much later date by 'the Crystal skull' in 2008. As well as filming in Utah for some of the desert scenes, Jordan, New Mexico and Colorado, several desert scenes were also shot in Spain in the Tabernas desert. Apparently the principal photography for 'Indiana Jones and the Last Crusade' began in Almeria in 1988, after many months of pre-production.

Obviously a bit of fakery went on with the filming of the Last Crusade. The city of Iskenderun — where the Holy Grail supposedly resides — is in south-east Turkey, but the makers presumed that any Arabic-looking city would do. And you don't get more Arabic-looking than Granada and the World Heritage-listed Alhambra, which was where several scenes were shot.

The railway station, where Dr Brody (Denholm Elliott) is besieged by beggars, is Guadix Station, Guadix, about thirty miles east of Granada, and the action scene where the plane crashes into the tunnel was actually filmed in the old mining town of Rodalquilar in the Natural Park of the Cabo de Gata-Nijar.

Stylish Place to Stay

Hotel Alhambra Palace, Granada,
Hotel Alhambra Palace Granada is situated on the top of the hill of the Alhambra overlooking the city. Only walking distance to the Arabians Palace. Inaugurated by His Majesty King Alfonso XIII on the first of January, 1910, and preserving the historic atmosphere, this building embraces grand aristocratic air and is filled with magnificent interiors. Every window, terrace and balcony overlooks the extraordinary beauty of the Sierra Nevada's ever-white peaks.

Delicious Place to Eat

Restaurante Las Tomasas, Granada
Housed in a 'Carmen' of the 19th century in the historical Moorish quarter of the Albaicin, this place offers unbelievable views of the Alhambra and the town of Granada. We particularly recommend the 'duck' which is simple but superb.

Genre: Action + Adventure
Destination: East Andalucia

Lawrence of Arabia (1962)

Lawrence of Arabia is a 1962 British film based on the life of T. E. Lawrence, starring Peter O'Toole, and directed by David Lean. It is widely considered one of the greatest and most influential films in the history of cinema.

While the famous desert scenes were mainly filmed in Jordan, ironically the Jordanian seaport of Aqaba wasn't deemed up to the task of playing itself. The seaport ended up being built from scratch on Playa del Algorocibo, near Carboneras. Many of the other cities and 'middle eastern' settings featured in David Lean's epic turned out to be Seville, though. The Cairo officer's club is the Palaio Espanol in Plaza de Espana, while the buildings around Plaza De Americas double as Jerusalem and the Casino de la Exposicion fills in for the town hall in Damascus. Finally the Casa de Piltaos in Seville was used for the meeting of Allenby and Lawrence. The Moorish influence on Andalucia's biggest city was the deciding factor.

Other aspects of the film were also set in eastern Andalucia such as the attack on the train which was filmed at Genovese Beach, San Jose on Cabo de Gata-Nijar and the Tabernas desert was also used for several scenes.

Stylish Place to Stay

**La Joya de Cabo de Gata,
Cabo de Gata National Park**
The farm consists of a hill of about one hectare that has been landscaped with native plants to convert the place into a miraculous oasis in the middle of the desert. There is an open air Jacuzzi, swimming pool in the style of a Roman Bath, solariums, open air showers amongst the vegetation and large, shaded areas to rest, read and relax in. There is also an Arabian Pavilion to relax in: an open air barbecue and picnic area together with a viewing point that looks down to the ocean. This place is a delight for those who love nature.

Delicious Place to Eat

Bitacora, Las Negras
Situated in the heart of the Cabo de Gata nature reserve, overlooking the nearby village of Las Negras and the Mediterranean. This restaurant is renowned for its refined authentic (but contemporary) cuisine and ranks among the best in the Almería region.

Focus On...
Madrid

Madrid stands at the very centre of Spain –geographically, culturally and politically. Madrid as a capital not only offers the culture and good times of a sophisticated, modern city but it also retains the charm and elegance of its early years. The power and glory of Madrid is reflected in its parks, plazas, boulevards. Among the variety of attractions in Madrid are the Prado Museum; the 19th century Villahermosa Palace now the Thyssen-Bornemizsa Museum; the Reina Sofia Art Centre showcasing more than 300 modern works by Dali, Miro & Picasso among others; the 18th century Royal Palace on the lovely Plaza de Oriente; the bustling Puerta del Sol with its many shops, restaurants and tapas bars; Rastro Market on one of the oldest outdoor markets in Europe; and Retiro Park for strolling while admiring local artists and buskers. However, the attraction to visit Madrid is not restricted to museums and plazas, but it's the football, shopping and nightlife for which this city is renowned. Home to the famous football stadium of 'Real Madrid FC' which is an institution in itself, is a popular haunt for football fans globally. The stadium located in the business district known as the 'Santiago Bernabeu Stadium' seats over 80,000 spectators and is one of Madrid's most visited attractions.

Madrid has had its fair share of cultural icons - surrealist genius Salvador Dalí lived in the city as a student, as did filmmaker Luis Buñuel and poet and dramatist Federico García Lorca. International stars like Antonio Banderas and Penelope Cruz made their reputations with Spain's leading director, Pedro Almodóvar, who first claimed the world's attention with Women on the Verge of a Nervous Breakdown (1988). Although Almodóvar is not from the city, he moved to Madrid when he was 16, where he studied cinematic art and made his now highly acclaimed films. His very first movie, Pepi, Luci, Bom and Other Girls on the Heap (1980) was set and filmed in Madrid. All About My Mother (1999) won Almodóvar the Best Director award at the 1999 Cannes Film Festival and Best Foreign Language Film at the 2000 Oscars. Talk to Her, released in 2002, has won numerous international awards, including a Golden Globe, and Volver (2006) was extremely well received too, with Broken Promises (2009) his latest release.

Another world class film 'Doctor Zhivago' which was famously set in Russia (the old Soviet Russia) had to be replicated in Madrid when the Soviets refused to permit the director to film the story in a country where the book had been banned. So, the filmmakers had to go to Spain to recreate Russia.

The best way to get around the city is by foot or tourist bus. Where you can visit some of the highlights such as the tapas Villa Rosa bar in the Plaza Santa Ana (which was the film location of Almodovar's 1991 film 'High Heels'); Museo del Jamon (which was used for Almodovar's 'Live Flesh' film), and the Segovia Aqueduct in Plaza Mayor which set the scene for film Matador (1985).

ⓘ Stylish Essentials

General Information

Spain Tourist Information
www.spain.info

Eurorail Tickets
www.raileurope.co.uk
T. +44 (0) 8448 484 064
(UK general reservations)

Iberia Airlines
www.iberia.com

Catalonia

General Tourist Information
www.barcelonaturisme.com

Delta Ebro Tourist Information
www.deltaebro.com

**Museu de Ciencies Naturals
(Natural History Museum)**
Parc de la Ciutadella
T. +34 (0) 93 319 69 12
Open: 10.00–18.30 Tue-Sat;
10.00–14.30 Sun

Talking Tourist Car
www.gotours.es
T. +34 (0) 932 691 792
E. barcelona@gocartours.com

Barcelona Aquarium
www.aquariumbcn.com
T. +34 (0) 93221 7474
Open: 9.30–23.00

Biking Around Barcelona
T. +34 (0) 656 356 300
E. info@barcelonabiking.com
Open: daily 10.00–20.00

Concert Spanish Guitar
Basilica Del Pi (Placa Del Pi 7)
www.poemasl.es
T. +34 (0) 647 514 513
Shows: 21.00 weekly

Tibidabo Amusement Park
www.tibidabo.es
Open: 12.00–23.00

Restaurant En Ville
www.envillebarcelona.es
T. +34 (0) 93 302 8467
Open: Evening dinner from 19.00

Hotel 1898
www.hotel1898.com
T. +34 (0) 93 552 95 52
E. 1898@nnhotels.com

Delta Hotel
www.deltahotel.es
T. +34 (0) 97 74800 46
E. deltah@dsi.es

El Cadell
Calle de Ramón i Cajal, 29
43580 , Deltebre - Spain
T. +34 (0) 977 48 08 01

Hotel Arts
www.hotelartsbarcelona.com
T. +34 (0) 93 221 1000

CDLC Bar & lounge
www.cdlcbarcelona.com
T. +34 (0) 932 240 470
E. info@cdlcbarcelona.com

West Andalucia

Seville Bullfighting
www.plazadetorosdelamaestranza.com
T. +34 (0) 954 501382
E. taquilla@plazadetorosdelamaes
tranza.com

Hacienda de San Rafael
www.haciendadesanrafael.com
T. +34 (0) 954 227 116
E. info@haciendadesanrafael.com

El Rinconcillo
Calle Gerona 40, Seville
www.elrinconcillo.es
T. +34 (0) 954 220 099

V Boutique Hotel
www.hotelv-vejer.com
T. +34 (0) 956 45 1757
E. info@hotelv-vejer.com

El Faro Restaurant
Calle San Felix 15, Cadiz
Near the Caleta beach & San
Sebastian Castle,
www.elfarodecadiz.com
T. +34 (0) 956 21 10 68
E. info@elfarodecadiz.com
Open: 13.00–16.00 and
20.00–00.00

East Andalucia

Alhambra Tourist Information
www.alhambra.org

Tabernas Desert Horse riding
www.desertridersspain.com
E. info@desertridersspain.com

Hotel Alhambra Palace
www.h-alhambrapalace.es
T. +34 (0) 958 22 14 68
E. reservas@h-alhambrapalace.es

Restaurante Las Tomasas
Carril de San Agustín
www.lastomasas.com
T. +34 (0) 958 224 108
E. contact@lastomasas.com
Open: Summer, Tues-Sat,
08.30–00.00. Winter, Weds-Sun,
14.00–23.30

La Joya de Cabo de Gata
www.lajoyadecabodegata.com
T. +34 (0) 619 15 95 87
E. reservas@lajoyadecabodegata.com

Bitacora
www.bitacora-cabodegata.es
T. +34 (0) 950 388 155
E. info@bitacora-cabodegata.es

Madrid

Real Madrid FC Tours
Santiago Bernabeu Stadium
www.realmadrid.com
T. +34 (0) 902 30 17 09

Villa Rosa bar
Plaza Santa Ana 15, Madrid
T. +34 (0) 915 213 689

Museo del Jamon
C/ Mayor 8, Madrid
www.museodeljamon.com
T. +34 (0) 915 314 550

Kefalonia sailing, courtesy of Dreamstime.

GREECE

Cyclades | Ionian Islands | Sporades | Athens

🏆 Why is this place so special?

The country of Greece is a paradise for travellers who are interested in culture, impressive scenery, history and of course getting away from it all. Greece which constitutes the Balkan Peninsula, is surrounded by thousand of little islands, in which less than 200 are inhabited. The islands of Mykonos, Santorini, Crete, Paros, Naxos and Rhodes with their beautiful beaches, restaurants, nightlife and archaeological sites have been popular for decades. Or lesser known islands like Sifnos, Lesvos, Kea that have always been attractive to those looking for a more quiet escape. The impressive historical sites such as the Acropolis and Delphi and Olympia and spiritual places like Meteora (where centuries old monasteries crown giant rocks), have also been attracting tourists for years.

Ever since 'Boy on a Dolphin' was shot in Greece in 1957, its sapphire seas, islands, whitewashed villages and cities have been the setting for nearly 90 international movies. A string of classics followed, including 'Never on Sunday', shot in 1960 in the port town of Piraeus and starring Melina Merkouri. Although it was set in Turkey, many of the scenes in her second hit movie, Topkapi, were shot in Rhodes. And in 1964, Anthony Quinn starred as Zorba the Greek, which was shot in Crete.

Roger Moore played James Bond in 'For Your Eyes Only' (1981), filmed in Meteora and Corfu. The hang gliding scene was shot at the monasteries of Meteora and the casino scene was shot at Corfu's Achillion Palace. Corfu was also the site of an underwater scene showing an ancient Greek temple with a giant turtle swimming around it.

Summer Lovers, starring Darryl Hannah and Peter Gallagher was filmed on the island of Santorini in 1982. Mykonos Grand Hotel And Resort, a member of the Small Luxury Hotels of the World, overlooks Ayios Yiannis beach, where the movie Shirley Valentine was filmed in 1989, starring Pauline Collins. The next major movie filmed in

From top. Athens Forum, Acropolis, Skopelos Port, Amorgos. All courtesy of Dreamstime.

Greece was 'Captain Corelli's Mandolin', in 2001, with Nicolas Cage and Penelope Cruz; it was shot in Kefallonia. The following year, the last scenes of Bourne Identity, starring Matt Damon, were filmed on the island of Mykonos.

In 2008, the musical Mamma Mia! brought instant fame to two previously little-known islands in the Northern Sporades, Skopelos and Skiathos, where Meryl Streep and Pierce Brosnan dance on Kastani beach. The jetty was constructed for the shoot. The most often-asked question as soon as the film was released, was 'where was the wedding scene filmed?' the answer is St. John of the Small Castle church, about an hour's scenic drive from the town of Skopelos. And in 2009, look for the first-ever movie shot at the Acropolis and Olympia. Nia Vardalos, star of 'My Big Fat Greek Wedding' was granted a rare exception to film scenes from her new movie, 'My Life in Ruins' at these and other ancient sites in Greece. Richard Dreyfuss is her co-star. Its no wonder Greece has become so popular for movie fans following the footsteps of their favourite stars.

🛫 Fast Facts

Capital: Athens.

Location: Southern Europe, bordering the Aegean Sea, Ionian Sea, and the Mediterranean Sea, between Albania and Turkey.

Population: 11, 262,000.

Religion: Greek Orthodox 98%, Muslim 1.3%, Other 0.7%.

Languages: Greek 100%.

Getting there and exploring around

Obviously the main method of getting to Greece is by air – all major European airlines fly to Athens on a daily basis, such as British Airways, Olympic Airways and Virgin Atlantic. Thessaloniki in northeastern Greece is an alternative for those who might like to make their way south but it has far fewer connecting flights to foreign cities. Less-expensive charters (such as Easyjet) operate in the summer from Belfast and Dublin to Athens, less frequently to Corfu, Crete, Mykonos, and Rhodes. From the USA scheduled airlines Olympic, Delta, US Air, and Continental fly directly non-stop from New York, Montreal and Toronto.

In addition, to arriving by plane, large ferry boats connect Italy with the west coast ports of Greece. Occasionally you can also catch a ferry from Cyprus, Egypt, Israel, and Turkey. Most ferries stop at Corfu and in summer, an occasional ship will also stop at Kefallonia. Train travel to Greece is also feasible; a Euro-rail pass is valid for connections all the way to Athens or Istanbul and includes the ferry service from Italy. Endless types of passes are now offered – long stays, short stays, and combinations with airlines too.

Yachting is also a great way to get to Greece. As the Greek islands make up a total of 20% of the total area, creating a coastline of more than 1500 kms, it is certainly feasible to sail from nearby Turkey. There are numerous companies where you can charter a yacht (crewed if you don't have the experience!) or a 'gullet' depending on how stylish you want to travel.

Greek trains are generally slow but are inexpensive and fairly pleasant and are a good option for getting around the mainland. The Hellenic State Railway (OSE) also offers bus service from stations adjacent to major train terminals. (Bus service is faster, but second-class train fare is nearly 50% cheaper, and trains offer more comfortable and scenic rides.)

Taxis are one of the most convenient means of getting about in Greece, especially in major cities. At some major tourist locales the fixed charges for rides to select destinations are posted (from an airport to the city centre, for instance).

Best time of year to visit

July and August are undoubtedly the most popular months to visit Greece. This is the time Greece is alive and kicking. It is very hot and busy and can be crowded in the holiday resorts as Greeks and foreign tourists head out of the cities for their holidays. Rooms are hard to find so you really do need to book ahead. This is a great time if you are young, like to meet up with lots of other young people, and the beaches, bars and nightclubs are at their busiest.

August 15th is the biggest holiday in the summer months. The islands are incredibly busy and ferries will be booked ahead as well as accommodation. Athens is empty in August as all the Greeks, head out to the islands and countryside for their holidays and so it is a great time to visit the capital city (if you can bear the heat while wondering the sights!)

May and September is probably the ideal time to visit Greece. The weather is perfect, still hot, but not unbearably so. The children are in school so it's quieter and the businesses on the islands are all still open and have more time for you. The historical sites are less crowded. There is still nightlife around, especially at weekends.

The beaches are quite empty, especially on weekdays. This is the time of year when you have more chance of just turning up on an island or somewhere and finding accommodation, and also getting better prices.

November to March can be quite cold and rainy. You will get some days which have clear blue skies and sunshine but still chilly. It can rain a lot and over the last few years Greece has had a fair amount of snow in winter, some villages become snowed in for a few days. A lot of the shops and businesses on the islands and holiday towns will be closed.

? Must know before you go

Dress for the occasion. Greeks are pretty well-dressed, although conservative (except on a beach) so consider what you wear in churches and visiting people's homes. Religious or not, most people wouldn't walk into a church half-naked.

Eating etiquette. When in a tavern or a bar you might be given a drink or a sweet and all you have to do is to thank the giver, or say cheers (yamas) and then you do not have to touch what you have been offered. Don't force yourself to drink ouzo or eat the sweet in order not to be rude, all you have to do is to say thanks.

The Evil Eye. The belief in the Evil Eye is an ancient superstition in many cultures around the Mediterranean Sea, Arabia, Turkey and India. The Evil Eye is believed to be a negative power we all carry within ourselves. If we stare too long on a person, animal or an object we may inflict damage through this power. It is often totally unconsciously, but the staring in itself often comes from admiration or envy, which are perfect channels for the Evil Eye. Whether the Evil Eye exists or not is a matter of belief, and arguing about it will lead nowhere. Many Greeks are just as convinced that it exists, as you are it isn't.

📷 Highlights

Nightlife in Mykonos. Sample the island's famed clubs and bars and party with a celebrity crowd.

Diving in the Cyclades. Explore the deep blue sea and the fabulous pristine reefs and marine life.

Island hopping the Sporades. Hire a private yacht or sailing boat and hop around the islands exploring some of the idyllic beaches.

Ancient sights of Athens. Perched on the hills of Athens, a visit to the historical Acropolis is a must.

★ Star Spotting

'Astra', located in Mykonos town, is a legendary bar and lounge created by the respected Greek jewellery designer Minas, with groovy modernist rooms. Rock stars like Keith Richards have been spotted hanging out here.

Genre: Action + Adventure
Destination: Cyclades

✈ Regional Information

The Cyclades islands are the most well known of the Greek Islands, and include Santorini and Mykonos which are the two most popular islands in Greece. Off the beaten track islands, such as the Amorgos, offer travellers a less touristy experience of Greece.

Santorini has a barren, rocky and dramatic landscape, unlike the rest of Greece which is mainly lush and green. The volcano is still active, and the last eruption was in 1950, causing an earthquake that destroyed many villages on the island. The island's official name is Thira and its main town, Fira, which is also the capital of the Cyclades islands. Today, Santorini is the only inhabited Caldera (volcano cauldron) in the world. Unlike other islands in Greece, the towns and villages sit densely on top of the massive cliffs of the Caldera and from a distance appear like snow capping the towering mountain tops. For travellers who love a bit of history, then a visit to Akrotiri is a must. This ancient town that was buried when the volcano erupted 3500 years ago. Archeologists are still excavating it, but you can walk around in the little street quarters and see the buildings as they were. For adventure lovers who love the outdoors, there are plenty of walking and biking trails, such as a two hour walk from Imerovigli to Fira, which offer spectacular views.

Mykonos, one of Greece's most famous destinations, is widely known for its intense night life. Mykonos gained fame in the late 1960s, when Aristotle and Jackie Onassis made frequent stops on their yacht. Since then, the island's distinct bright-white buildings and mazelike alleyways have drawn fashion and entertainment celebs—Jean-Paul Gaultier, Gianfranco Ferre, Sean 'Diddy' Combs. The island allocates an incredible folk architecture, a splendid naked landscape, exceptional climate, a lot of beautiful sandy coasts and has the privilege to be located near to the 'Open Archeological Museum' of Delos, the island of Apollo.

Hora is the capital of Mykonos, with 3,500 inhabitants. Apart to the Municipality of Mykonos the island also has a Village, called Ano Mera, which arises the total population to 4,000 residents. Most of the bars and clubs are based in Chora. There are also beach parties going on all through the summer so keep a lookout for advertising posters. Night parties can go on until the morning and be continued in the famous beach bars of Mykonos like Cavo Paradiso and Tropicana in Paradise beach, Super Paradise bar, in Super Paradise beach, Sol Y Mar in Kalo livadi, and Elia bar in Elia beach.

Amorgos is by no means a commercialised island, though, and it is truly an incredible place for relaxing, with its stark white houses, crystal clear water and a peaceful atmosphere: it is no coincidence that Luc Besson chose to shoot the first part of The Big Blue here. Once only visited by the occasional backpacker, Amorgos has become quite an 'trendy' island since the film was released, and it is no surprise that you will find more French holidaymakers here than usual. Even though it is a very small island, there are quite a few things to see. The locals are very friendly and they are working hard to make the island look its best at the beginning of each season. The capital, Chora, is a very quiet village with about 500 inhabitants. It is situated high up in the mountains, and the road is long and winding. Even though it is so small, there are quite a few little taverns and cafes. This is truly a place where the time has stopped, and thanks to local regulations, the architecture is kept in the traditional style. There is a church attached to the cliff, and the locals are also proud to have Greece's smallest church here - with room for only three. There is also a museum as well as a Venetian Citadel from the 13th century, which is worth a visit.

Katapola is a village next to the sea with lovely little fish taverns along the harbour. From here you can get to the monastery Chozoviotissa, which according to tradition it was built in the 9th century after a ship had sunk just outside Amorgos carrying an icon of the Virgin Mary, or Panagia (all saint) as she is called in Greek. With a little luck the monks will offer you some local liqueur.

Getting around the Cylcades is fairly easy, with regular ferry trips which take four to five hours to the closest islands (Kythnos, Syros, Tinos, Mykonos, Sifnos) and from eight to ten hours to the furthest (Santorini) depending on how many stops it makes. The highspeed ferries take half the time but cost twice as much. There are daily ferries from Pireaus to all these islands, with the exception of Kea which you get to from Lavrion and Andros which you get to from Rafina.

Genre: Action + Adventure
Destination: Cyclades

🎬 The Bourne Identity (2002)

The 2002 action, spy film, often referred to as the 'new James Bond' is very loosely based on Robert Ludlum's novel of the same name, and the first of three films in the Bourne Series. It stars Matt Damon as Jason Bourne, a psychogenic amnesiac attempting to discover his true identity amidst a clandestine conspiracy within the CIA to track him down and arrest or kill him for inexplicably failing to carry out an officially unsanctioned assassination and then failing to report back in afterwards. Along the way he teams up with Marie, played by Franka Potente, who assists him on the initial part of his journey to learn about his past and regain his memories. The film was shot on several well-known locations such as Paris, Prague and the Liguria coastline but the final scenes were shot on Mykonos, where Bourne finally tracks down Marie (his love interest in the film) to the Greek island, where she's running a scooter rental business at Sea Satin Market in Little Venice, beneath the island's famous windmills.

🛏 Stylish Place to Stay

Ostraco Suites, Mykonos

This funky retreat sits on a hill above the impossibly pretty horseshoe-harbour of Chora, with long views out to a scudding blue sea. Guests lounge around on sumptuously cushioned day-beds in bamboo-shaded pergolas, or top up their tans on white-clad sun loungers around an amoeba-shaped pool. In the evening, the place comes alive with music, lanterns, cocktails and a party-soul bartender: a fitting prelude for a night on the tiles of Chora's labyrinthine alleys, glitzy restaurants and laid-back dance clubs.

🍽 Delicious Place to Eat

Kiki's, Mykonos

A taverna without a sign or phone number, Kiki's is perched above the beach and hidden behind the trees that surround it. The simple menu includes Greek salads and the fish of the day. During peak lunch hours (from 3 to 5pm in Mykonos), the outdoor tables fill up quickly.

Genre: Action + Adventure
Destination: Cyclades

Le Grand Bleu (1988)

A visionary epic of obsession and beauty about Jacques Mayol, the handsome diver who is so at home in the water, that he seems only half-human. Jacques' best friends are a family of playful porpoises and Enzo Molinari, his swaggering Italian diving rival. Jacques and Enzo grew up together in the Mediterranean, and remain lifelong friends despite a fierce battle for the top prize in the world free diving championships, where divers compete to see who can descend to the furthest depths of the sea with no equipment other than their own courage and determination. But when the dreamer Jacques falls in love with the beautiful Johanna, he finds himself torn between the damsel and the deep blue sea.

Filming took place in France, Italy and Peru. The stranded boat is on Amorgos, where there was filming at the Grand Bleu bar and also on Manganari (where Luc Besson the films director) spent some of his childhood and which also inspired the film.

Luc Besson fell in love with Amorgos & decided to shoot a great deal of the movie on the island. Chora, Agia Anna & the shipwreck which are the main sights that the story takes place are by far not by chance selected.

Stylish Place to Stay

Karkisia Hotel, Amorgos
A locally owned, friendly hotel, situated a 2 minute walk from the main town Aegiali, with stunning views over the harbour and of neighbouring island Nicouria. All the rooms are spacious with little kitchenettes and balconies. The amazing bakery nearby is also not to be missed!

Delicious Place to Eat

Kamara Café, Amorgos
Located in Potamos, with a panoramic restaurant and café, it offers peace and a spectacular view of Aefiali's bay. The cuisine is definitely traditional, using plenty of local ingredients (such as Goat) and they even offer Greek cookery classes in May, September and October.

Genre: Epics + Historical
Destination: Ionian Islands

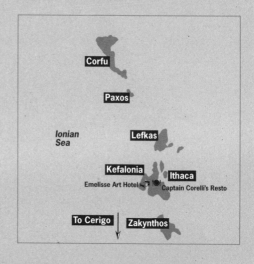

Corfu

Paxos

Ionian
Sea

Lefkas

Kefalonia

Ithaca

Emelisse Art Hotel — Captain Corelli's Resto

To Cerigo

Zakynthos

✈ Regional Information

It's hard not to fall for the Ionian Islands, an archipelago that sweeps down the west
coast of mainland Greece. Their natural beauty embraces everyone– the vast olive
groves, intriguing landscapes and iridescent waters of the Ionian Sea offer something
for adventure seekers, culture vultures and beach bums. There are seven islands which
form part of the group, these being, Kerkyra usually known as Corfu in English, Paxi
also known as Paxos, Lefkada also known as Lefkas, Ithaki, known as Ithaca, Kefalonia,
Zakynthos sometimes known as Zante and Kythira sometimes known as Cerigo in
English. All the islands have their own unique identities, from the green valleys of
Kefalonia, charming villages of Ithaca, to the white beaches of Lefkada.

The two best-known islands are Corfu, one of the first places in Greece to attract
package holidaymakers in the 1960s, and Kefalonia which unwittingly acquired an army
of fans worldwide especially after the production of Captain Corelli's Mandolin.

Zakynthos is another popular package holiday destination whilst those seeking
a tranquil island untouched by mass tourism head for unspoilt Ithaca, the legendary
kingdom of Odysseus. Lefkada offers bustling tourist resorts along with many wonderful
walking trails and traditional mountain villages.

The Ionian archipelago is quite different from the Aegean islands in terms of
both its culture and appearance. You'll find many legacies of the French and British
occupations here rather than the Turkish influence which is so much in evidence on the
Aegean islands. Corfu boasts the only cricket ground in Greece and eager local teams
still turn up in their whites for regular matches.

The Ionian islands receive above average rainfall (Corfu has the highest rainfall in
the whole of Greece) with the result that they're lush and green, awash with olive groves,
cypresses and mountainsides carpeted with orchids and other wild flowers in springtime.

Genre: Epics + Historical
Destination: Ionian Islands

Kefalonia, made famous as the setting for Captain Corelli's Mandolin, is one of the most beautiful settings in the Ionian Sea. With its supremely panoramic views from the towering Mount Enos, Kefalonia reveals a glimpse of paradise at every turn. From churches and monasteries perched precariously on cliff tops to secluded sandy coves and timeless, untouched villages - you'll find an abundance of spectacular scenery, traditional tavernas, perfumed pine forests, stunning white beaches and warm, friendly Greek Island hospitality.

Native to Kefalonia are some of the best beaches in the Greek islands, with waters considered amongst the cleanest in the world. Much of the busy nightlife in Kefalonia is concentrated in the main holiday town of Argostoli.

The central square is lined with many restaurants, cafés and bars, and on a hot, balmy summer night local people take their traditional evening walk here. Kefalonia's larger harbour side resorts also offer bustling entertainment, including traditional dancing and live Greek music. In the smaller, more rural villages you'll find local tavernas and nightspots offering a quieter, relaxing and romantic evening retreat.

Acres of inland forest-covered mountains provide captivating views of Kefalonia and its stunning scenery – neighbouring Greek Island Zakynthos can even be spotted on a clear blue-sky day. Spend the day visiting tiny isolated beaches and coves all along Kefalonia's pretty coastline on a boat trip; observe the sea-turtles nesting on the beach, and visit natural wonders like sinkholes that make sea water disappear then reappear across Kefalonia island. Horseback riding is found at several holiday resorts, as well as watersports facilities, cycle hire and bird watching hotspots.

Archaeological finds suggest that humans lived in Kefalonia since Neolithic times 7,000 years ago. For the explorer, many ancient sites of unrivalled beauty still reside here. These range from Venetian fortresses and monasteries, Byzantine churches and underground Mycenaean tombs dating back to 1200 BC, to the remains of a Roman villa and its fascinating mosaics from the second century AD. More recently, visitors flock to this Greek Island for its connection to Captain Corelli's Mandolin – the book, and subsequent film, inspired by World War.

Genre: Epics + Historical
Destination: Ionian Islands

Captain Corelli's Mandolin (2001)

Kefalonia was buzzing in the summer of 2000 with film crews and the actors Nicholas Cage, Penelope Cruz and John Hurt who are starring in the film Captain Corelli's Mandolin. Most of the filming took place in Sami - and the surrounding hills.

Literature and film-lovers can retrace the steps of Captain Corelli in Sami, and visit the stunning Antisamos and Myrtos (Mirtos) bays and beaches. Other popular beaches on Kefalonia include Petani, Emblisi, Foki, Skala, Avithos, and Trapezaki.

The old town was re-created especially for the story. It brought back both happy and sad memories for the people of Kefalonia who endured the war time occupation on Kefalonia. The exposure Kefalonia received as a result of the film meant the island has an increasing number of tourists visiting it each year. Kefalonia was put on the map in 2000 and the island has never been busier since.

Stylish Place to Stay

Emelisse Art Hotel, Kefalonia

This romantic bolthole is beautifully positioned along the rugged shoreline of Kefalonia. Care has been taken over every detail at the hotel. Everything is effortlessly stylish, from the deep sofas that surround the pool and look out over the magnificent azure ocean, to the rain-like showers in the rooms. At night the hotel is lit by soft lamps and candlelight, transforming it into a romantic spot, so you can snuggle up on a plush sofa or on one of the numerous expansive terraces.

Delicious Place to Eat

Captain Corelli's Restaurant, Kefalonia

During the summer of 2000 this Cafe - Restaurant was the meeting place for all the important people that took part in the shooting of the film (Nicolas Cage, Penelope Cruz, John Hurt, John Tole, John Madden, Irene Papas and many others). Hence, they gave it the name 'Captain Corelli's'. Whilst the dining experience may not be top notch cuisine, this is a friendly place offering typical Greek wines, and dishes such as lamb moussaka.

Genre: Musicals
Destination: Sporades

✦ Regional Information

Sporades is the group of islands that located in the north east of Evia and the peninsula of mount Pelion of Magnesia prefecture in central Greece. The islands that are included in this group are the islands of Skiathos, Skopelos, Alonissos and Skyros being the largest one. The Sporades are a popular holiday destination for Greeks and foreign tourists, and have some of the best beaches in Greece. All of the Sporades islands are very Green and during the summer they have relatively more mild temperatures then other Greek islands mainly caused by their location and their nature. The islands of the Sporades have some of the best beaches in Greece.

Skiathos is one of the few islands in Greece that has never changed name. It is not certain where the name comes from and one theory has it that it is a pre-Greek name given to the island's very first inhabitants. Another explanation is that it comes from the Greek word for shadow, Skia, and that it got it because of its many trees, or that the island lies in the shadow of the mountains of Pelion on the mainland. Prehistoric findings on Skiathos tell us that the island has been inhabited since pre-historic times. Skiathos has a tradition of shipbuilding, and together with the fertile soil it became an important resting place for expeditions and travellers. It is believed that both the Greek fleet against Troy, as well as Jason and the Argonauts made a stop here before sailing on.

Genre: Musicals
Destination: Sporades

Many visitors think Skopelos is the prettiest island of the Sporades, or even Greece, since the buildings are old and white, with huge bougainvillea and flowerpots, it's full of churches (apparently 360 of them!) and it is completely covered with forest. The landscape is dramatic, with high mountains and deep valleys. Although the island has been marketed by most major tour operators as a quiet island best suited for couples and families. This is not completely true, since there are many bars and quite a few clubs on the island, especially in Chora, its capital. It is not a place for partying all day and all night, but there is quite a good nightlife in a jazzy, sophisticated way.

Alonissos has been inhabited from prehistoric times, and it was the object of a number of disputes over it, especially between Athens and Macedonia. Patitiri, the capital of the island, offers a variety of transportation services connecting the island with the other islands nearby and the mainland. There are beautiful locations around Patitiri, such as Rousoum village, which has one of the most beautiful beaches. It was conquered by the Romans in the 2nd century AD, and then the Byzantines arrived, who built the walls of the castle of Chorio, and left a set of awesome buildings which were unfortunately torn down by the frequent earthquakes on the island. After the Byzantines, several other peoples ruled the island, such as the Venetians, and the Turks in 1538. Alonissos became part of Greece in 1830. Today Alonissos is the most serene of the northern Sporades Islands, and still quite untouched by tourism, which is growing at a slow pace.

Skyros, although the largest of the Sporades is arguable the most traditional of the islands, full of local culture, and it remains far from commercial in terms of tourism. Visitors will be impressed with the dedication of the Skyrians to their traditional inheritance. The dedication shows through happenings, such as the big Skyrian Carnival, a traditional street festival called Apokries or 'Goat Dance' carnival leading up to Easter, as much as through the traditional art of the island with the significant embroideries, ceramics and wood engravings. Skyros capital is dominated by its kastro (a Byzantine fortress), which is open to visitors. There was probably an acropolis here already in the Bronze age, but the current fortification dates back to the Venetian rule. There is an archaeological museum here, as well as folklore museum which both hold interesting finds and objects from the island. If you're spending a week or so hopping the islands then spending a couple of days exploring the Skyros culture and beaches would make a trip to the Sporades unique.

Genre: Musicals
Destination: Sporades

🎬 Mama Mia! (2007)

The movie version of the hit stage show Mamma Mia! was the summers' number one screening, and a definite must-see for anyone who is passionate about Greece. The little Greek islands of Skopelos and Skiathos, in the Northern Sporades, were almost unheard of until the release of the box-office record-breaker.

The film tells the story of 18-year-old Sophie (Amanda Seyfried) who has a problem. It's almost her wedding day and she doesn't know who her father is. It could be any of her mother Donna's (Meryl Streep) past suitors: Sam Carmichael (Pierce Brosnan), Bill Austin (Stellan Skarsgard) or Harry Bright (Colin Firth).

The plot may not be the most complex, but the islands' eye-catching landscapes are memorable enough to entice travellers away from the usual suspects of Mykonos, Santorini and Patmos – or to lure visitors who have never been to the Greek islands before.

Filming primarily took place on Skopelos and Skiathos, with some shots in coastal town of Damouchari in Greece's Pelion region. The smaller, off-the beaten track beaches, coves and harbours of Skopelos and Skiathos play a starring role in the movie. Perivoli, on the sparsely inhabited north coast, with jagged rocks and windswept flora, was used for many scenes, which can be reached by taxi or hire car and combined with a few hours in nearby Glossa.

One of the Mamma Mia! crew's famous hang-outs was Limnonari, which is a scenic 15 minute walk from Agnondas with no bus access. The white-sand beach, flanked by forested hills, is an excellent place to laze in relative seclusion - but with tavernas nearby.

The cast and crew were also spotted eating out at various local restaurants including to Klimataria, Tis Annas, The Garden (Skopels Town), Agioli (Skipelos Village Hotel) and Agnanti restaurant in Glossa

🛏 Stylish Place to Stay

Mandraki Boutique Hotel, Skiathos

This cosy boutique hotel is where the cast and crew allegedly stayed while filming in Skiathos. Each bungalow has its own private entrance, with beautiful stunning gardens as views. It's situated 200 only metres from Koukounaries beach, on the protected area of the Strofilia Lake, making it an enviable location for those looking to get away from it all.

🍽 Delicious Place to Eat

Ouzeria Anatoli, Skopelos

One of the liveliest tavernas in Skopleos, its simple style situated within the low-walled ruins of the Venetian citadel at the highest point of Skopelos town. Rustic food, local wine, wide views and sea air combine to awesome effect with Rembetika songs (Greek folk songs) played by the musician-owner. Open until the early hours of the morning.

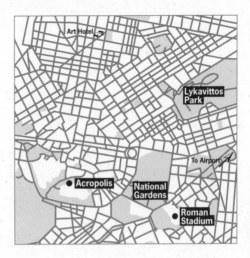

Focus On...
Athens

Athens really seems to have it all. Fabulous archaeological ruins, mystical museums, crazy nightlife, shopping and all night cafes. It's no wonder travellers seem to flock here, not only for a long weekend break but as a starting point to a longer Greek adventure.

What would a visit to this classical city be without going to the Acropolis and the Parthenon? You can take a tour or wander up there yourself but during the summer, whatever you do, unless it is overcast, go early or late in the day. It can get very hot up there and gasping for breath can take way from your ability to marvel at the greatest of all archaeological sites. Obviously you can do this with or without the help of a 'tour guide', of which there are plenty surrounding the area.

'My life in ruins' (2009) a comedy film, starring Nia Vardalos, which was famously shot in and around the Acropolis, shares the story of an American academic who has taken a job as a 'tour guide' in Athens after losing her teaching job. There are the drinking Australians, the fussbudget Brits, the nice Canadians who melt into the scenery, the hot, divorced Spanish ladies, and those loud, stupid or boring Americans. A lone Yank exception is Irv (Richard Dreyfuss), a grieving widower who experiences visions of his late wife (Rita Wilson), but who, wise as his years, dispenses good advice of which Georgia is benefactor. The film shows off Greece's magnificent scenery and cultural life.

Athens isn't just famous for its 'ruins' but increasingly its nightlife, with everything ranging from Rembetika music clubs, to tavernas with live music and rock clubs.
A range of newly opened sophisticated hotels have also paved the way for 'fashion style' cafes, such as the Semiramis boutique hotel and Art hotel, which are funky and draw in young crowds.

ⓘ Stylish Essentials

General Information

General Tourist Information
www.visitgreece.gr

Greek National Tourist Office
www.gnto.co.uk
T. +44 (0) 20 7495 9300
Enquiries & Information
E. info@gnto.co.uk

Olympic Airlines
www.olympicairlines.com
T. +30 210 9666666
(telephone sales)
E. olympicairlines.telephone.sales@
olympicairlines.gr

ANEK Lines Ferry Company
www.anek.gr

**Paleologos Agency's
Ferry's across Greece**
www.ferries.gr

Viamare Travel
Graphic House, 2 Sumatra Rd,
London
NW6 1PU
www.viamare.com
T. + 44 (0) 870 410 6040

Superfast Ferries Line
157 Leoforos Alkyonidon,
16673 Athens
www.superfast.com
T. +30 210 969 1100

Rail Europe
www.raileurope.co.uk
T. +44 (0) 8448 484 064
General Reservations

Seascape Sailing
Leros Marina
Lakki, Leros 85400
Greece
www.seascape-sail.com
T. + 30 6944 740 649
F. +30 211 268 6569

Cyclades

General Tourist Information
www.iles-cyclades.com

Santorini Tourist Information
www.santorini.com

Santorini VIP Tours
www.santoriniviptours.com
Limousines', private Helicopter
services
T. +30 6978 131330

Scuba Diving in Naxos
Agia Ana, Plaka
www.naxosdiving.com
T. +30 2285042072

Ostraco Suites
www.ostraco.gr
T. +30 22890 23396
E. info@ostraco.gr

Kiki's Restaurant
Agios Sostis Beach,
north side of Mykonos,
just past Panormos Bay.

Karkisia Hotel
www.karkisia-hotel.gr
T. +30 22850 731 80

Kamara Café
www.kamaracafe.com
T. +30 228 5073 260
E. kamaracafe@yahoo.gr

Ionian Islands

**General Tourist Information
Kefalonia**
www.justkefalonia.co.uk
T. +30 26950 52141

Captain Corelli's Day Tour
Kefalonia
www.ainostravel.gr
Every Saturday

Sailing Ionian Islands
Sailing trips & yacht charter
www.ionianbluesailing.co.uk
T. +44 (0) 1793 538 718
E. info@ionianbluesailing.co.uk

Emelisse Art Hotel
www.arthotel.gr/emelisse/
T. +30 26740 41200
E. emelisse@arthotel.gr

Captain Corelli's Restaurant
Agia Efimia,
Port of Sami,
Kefalonia

Sporades

Hydrofoil Company
Hellenic Seaways
www.hellenicseaways.gr
T. +30 210 419 900

Yacht Charter Skiathos
Odyssey sailing
www.odysseysailing.gr
T. +30 24210 36676

Skopelos Walking tours
www.skopelos-walks.com
T. + 30 24240 24022

Skiathos Tourist Information
www.travel-to-skiathos.com
T. +30 210 4101130

Mandraki Boutique Hotel
www.mandraki-skiathos.gr
T. +30 24270 49301
E. info@mandraki-skiathos.gr

Ouzeria Anatoli Taverna
Skopelos Town
Open: Day and night

Athens

Athens & Acropolis Tours
www.hopin.com
T. + 30 210 428 5500
E. adm@hopin.com

Athens walking tours
www.athenswalkingtours.gr
T. +30 210 8847269
E. info@athenswalkingtours.gr

Semiramis Hotel
www.semiramisathens.com

Ambelofilo
Light Greek Island music.
Traditional Greek food.
3 Karagiani & Samothrakis, Kypseli.
T. +30 210 8678862

Rembetiki Istoria
Authentic rembetika by Pavlos
Vasileiou and his band.
181 Ippokratous Street, Excarchia,
Athens
T. +30 210 6424937
Open: Every day but closed on
Mondays.

Stoa Athanaton
Old time Rembetika singers including
some heroes of the past.
Sofokleos 19 in the Athens Central
Meat Market.
Open: 15.30–19.30 and at night.
Closed Sunday.

Privilege
Nightclub & bar
Peraios 130 and Alkesonios. Gazi.
T. +30 210 347 7311

Art Hotel Athens
www.arthotelathens.gr
T. +30 210 524 0501

Sabi Sands, Kruger National Park.

SOUTH AFRICA

Johannesburg | Kwazulu-Natal | Soweto | Cape Town

SOUTH AFRICA ● ● ●

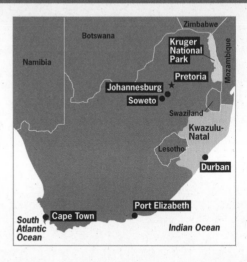

Zimbabwe
Botswana
Namibia
Kruger National Park
Mozambique
Pretoria
Johannesburg
Soweto
Swaziland
Kwazulu-Natal
Lesotho
Durban
Port Elizabeth
South Atlantic Ocean
Cape Town
Indian Ocean

🏆 Why is this place so special?

South Africa is one of the world's most diverse countries. Featuring cosmopolitan cities like Cape Town, stunning natural panoramas such as Table Mountain and vibrant cultures, make it appealing to almost every taste and budget. It is made up of 9 different provinces; Western Cape, Eastern Cape, Northern Cape, Free State, North West, Gauteng, Limpopo, Mpumalanga and KwaZulu Natal, all offering an independent traveller a variety of experiences from hiking in Drakensburg mountains to sipping wine in Stellenbosch.

South Africa may also be well known for its wonderful game parks and spotting the 'big 5'; but it is also home to 7 World Heritage Sites. The Cradle of Humankind containing thousands of fossils of animal, and Stone Age artefacts; The Greater St Lucia Wetland Park, with five distinct eco systems and boasts a spectacular diversity of plant life, animals and bird species. Robben Island, only a short boat trip from the V&A waterfront in Cape Town, and famous for its holding political prisoner 'Nelson Mandela'. uKhahlamba or Drakensberg Park as its also known, which is a mountainous area of outstanding natural beauty and wealth of evidence of early life, earned this area its title. Mapungubwe, declared a World Heritage Site in 2003, this Iron Age site was the centre of the largest kingdom in Southern Africa, where gold and ivory were traded to the East. The Cape Floral Kingdom, found at the Cape Peninsula and on Table Mountain is one of only 6 floral kingdoms in the world. As this area is under constant threat from development it was declared a World Heritage Site only recently. The seventh World Heritage site is the Vredefort Dome 120km south-west of Johannesburg, is a large crater - which has a radius of 190km - in the Free State which was created when a giant meteor struck the area some 2 billion years ago.

South Africa has a long history of film making, beginning with the shooting of the first-ever newsreels during the Anglo-Boer War at the turn of the previous century.

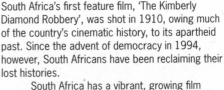

From top. Shangan dancers. Game drive, Kruger. Cape Point.

South Africa's first feature film, 'The Kimberly Diamond Robbery', was shot in 1910, owing much of the country's cinematic history, to its apartheid past. Since the advent of democracy in 1994, however, South Africans have been reclaiming their lost histories.

South Africa has a vibrant, growing film industry that is increasingly competitive internationally. Local and foreign filmmakers are taking advantage of the country's diverse, unique locations – as well as low production costs and favourable exchange rate, which make it up to 40% cheaper to make a movie here than in Europe or the US.

A string of successful big budget productions have been filmed here, including Blood Diamond with Leonardo DiCaprio and Lord of War, starring Nicholas Cage as a global arms dealer. Lord of War showcases South Africa's wealth of breathtaking locations - with Cape Town appearing as 57 different settings in the Middle East, Afghanistan, Bolivia, and Sierra Leone. Big budget films aside, South Africa will surely be 'on the map' for many travellers, during and after the FIFA World Cup 2010.

🛖 Fast Facts

Capital: Pretoria (administrative capital).

Location: On the very southern tip of Africa, and is surrounded by two oceans, Indian Ocean and Atlantic Ocean. Neighbouring countries are Mozambique, Namibia, Swaziland, Zimbabwe, Botswana and Lesotho.

Population: 49 million.

Religion: Christianity 75%; no religious affiliation 21%; Muslim, Hindu and Jewish 4%.

Languages: 11 official languages. English is the most commonly spoken, followed by Afrikaans, Zulu and Xhosa.

✈ Getting there and exploring around

The major air hubs for South Africa, and for the entire surrounding region, is Johannesburg and Cape Town offering numerous direct flights from Europe, is becoming an increasingly important gateway. The smaller Durban International Airport handles several regional flights, as does Mpumalanga Kruger International Airport near Nelspruit and Kruger National Park.

South African Airways is the national airline, with an excellent route network and safety record. In addition to its international routes, it operates regional flights together with its subsidiaries South African Airlink and South African Express.

Buses in South Africa aren't the deal that they are in many other countries. A good alternative to standard bus lines is Baz Bus which caters almost exclusively to backpackers and other travellers. It offers hop-on, hop-off fares and door-to-door service between Cape Town and Jo'burg via the Northern Drakensberg, Durban and the Garden Route. It also has a loop service from Durban via Zululand and Swaziland to Jo'burg, passing close by Kruger National Park.

South Africa is ideal for driving, and away from the main bus and train routes, having your own wheels is the best way to get around. Most major roads are in excellent condition, and off the main routes there are interesting back roads to explore. Driving is on the left-hand side of the road, as in the UK, Japan and Australia.

Although South Africa has a horrific road-accident record, the N1 between Cape Town and Beaufort West is considered to be the most dangerous stretch of road in the country. The main hazards are your fellow drivers, though animals and pedestrians on the roads are another hazard, especially in rural areas.

Car rental is relatively inexpensive in South Africa. For cheaper rates and unlimited mileage deals, it's best to book and prepay through your agent at home before coming to South Africa.

Getting around by train is also an option. If you want to really splash out then take the very luxurious 'Blue Train' (which offers services from Cape Town to Pretoria as well as other routes), your private butler will be at your service offering you unlimited alcohol, 4 course dinner and even run you a bath!

Private planes are expensive but offer a thrilling experience, and are quick and easy to get to the game parks. Usually you can book through the private game parks when you book your accommodation.

☼ Best time of year to visit

A South African safari is possible any time of year since extremes in weather are tempered by maritime conditions at southerly latitudes. Each season offers a different game viewing experience. Spring and summer (September- February), generally classed as 'high season' are the rainy season that turns the bush green, lush and thick. Newborn animals are best spotted during this time. Autumn and winter (March-August) are dry months when the bush is less dense and water is more precious. This is prime season to quietly watch animals gather at the waterholes or along riverbanks. It is always advisable to take a warm jacket, as temperatures can get very cold at night.

The eastern shores of the KwaZulu-Natal coast have a subtropical climate with warm humid weather year round. The winter months of June and July are ideal to visit this region, which is rich in marine and bird life and boasts some fabulous beaches. Along the Garden Route and around Cape Town, the weather is famous for being unpredictable throughout the year. So if you're planning to hike up 'table mountain' then take lots of layers, or better still hire a private guide for the day.

? Must know before you go

Health risks. Many of the main tourism areas are malaria-free, so you need not worry at all. However, the Kruger National Park and the northern part of KwaZulu-Natal do pose some low risk for malaria, so consult your travel clinic before you go.

Visiting in low season. The dry season is the best time to see wildlife in the great national parks and the private game reserves of the Eastern Cape. The bush is less dense, so you can spot the animals more easily, especially around the waterholes where nature leads them to gather. Great names such as Kruger and Mpumalanga beckon. Plus it's a lot cheaper!

Take care in townships. South Africa has some of the highest violent crime rates in the world but by being vigilant and using common sense you should have a safe and pleasant trip - as hundreds of thousands of people have each year. Stick to general safety precautions e.g. don't walk around in deserted areas at night, like the townships which should be visited with a reputable tour guide; and don't advertise money and expensive jewellery.

Highlights

Safari in style. Take a light aircraft from Johannesburg to a luxury safari in Kruger, and spot the big '5' on a game drive.

Explore the mountains. Take helicopter ride to view the Drakensberg Mountains or better still hike it.

Experience the townships. Visit Soweto, the biggest, most vibrant township in South Africa and take a peek inside Nelson Mandela's first house.

Visit the vineyards. The Stellenbosch Wine Route is arguably the country´s most famous, and has 106 cellars - most of which are open to the public, located just outside Cape Town.

★ Star Spotting

Head to the V&A waterfront in Cape Town, where you are sure to spot a few local and international film stars like Charlize Theron having lunch in one of the fine restaurants.

Genre: Epics + Historical
Destination: Johannesburg

✈ Regional Information

Often referred to as the 'City of Gold' due its to rich gold-mining heritage, or simply 'Jo'burg', Johannesburg is a striking city, filled with contrast and considerable wealth, despite its relative youth, being founded just over 120 years ago, in 1886. The Johannesburg of today is South Africa's financial capital and a truly vast city, being one of the biggest in the whole of Africa, after only Cairo and also Lagos.

Johannesburg offers some of the worlds most pristine garden suburbs, while urban streetscapes flaunt a wealth of Victorian, Edwardian, Art Deco, Modernist and International architectural styles. Outside of the cities a naturally rugged landscape, interspersed with agricultural farmland.

Johannesburg boasts many sights to see, with the Gandhi Square and the very spacious Nelson Mandela Square standing out. Also of note is the Constitution Hill, where the Johannesburg Constitutional Court is located, as well as the prison that once housed famously both Mahatma Gandhi and also Nelson Mandela.

A trip to the very historical Johannesburg Zoo is also recommended, as is an afternoon at the Gold Reef City, where you will find an authentic reconstruction of how the city appeared during the gold rush of the late 19th century. For the very best views, head to the Top of Africa skyscraper building and enjoy a meal at its rooftop restaurant.

Just outside Johannesburg there is plenty to keep travellers busy. The majestic Magaliesburg mountain range is a thirty minute drive from Johannesburg and offers distinctive scenic and dramatic vistas. Across much of the region gold mines and mining villages, both historic and operational, dot the landscape while undulating savannah-like grasslands and numerous nature reserves holding all manner of wildlife are within convenient reach. The extensive and well-preserved cave formations of Sterkfontein and Kromdraai are found within the Cradle of Humankind, a UNESCO World Heritage site of global significance.

While going to Magaliesburg a visit to the Hartbeespoort Dam is a must. It is one of the popular tourist attractions in Magaliesburg. Here you can indulge in various types of adventurous sports like jet-skiing, para-sailing, wind surfing, hot air ballooning, paragliding and hang gliding. The Hartbeespoort Dam houses a snake park, zoo, cable way and an aquarium.

Just an hour by plane will take you to the famous and spectacular Kruger National Park, one of the largest game reserves in South Africa, and where you can safari in luxury and spot the 'big 5.' There are numerous private reserves which offer all kinds of accommodation from rest camps, to lodges with roaring fires suites with private plunge pools.

For those who miss out on the big cats, there is a 'lion park' near Johannesburg, where you can experience getting up close and personal with lion cubs. The park cares for and breeds indigenous lion species, including the rare white lion. It is also home to many of the other animals that make South Africa one of the wildlife jewels of the world. You can also get involved with feeding and caring for the big cats, keeping their environment clean and maintaining the park.

Genre: Epics + Historical
Destination: Johannesburg

🎬 Skin (2009)

Elysian films produced the international feature film, Skin, which is one of the most bizarre and fascinating true stories to emerge from South Africa in recent times. Sandra Laing (Sophie Okonedo) was a coloured child born in the 1950s to two white Afrikaners, unaware of their black ancestry. The film follows Sandra's thirty-year journey from rejection to acceptance, betrayal to reconciliation, as she struggles to define her place in a changing world — and triumphs against all odds. Her father Abraham (Sam Neill) is having a particularly difficult time accepting his daughter. Despite the fact that tests indicate he is her biological father, the neighbours constantly whisper behind their backs. And while Sandra's mother (Alice Kreig) does her best to provide her daughter with understanding and emotional support, those consolations come at a high price for both mother and daughter. Whilst the storyline is compelling and fascinating, the film also shows some of South Africa's stunning countryside. Shot in and around Johannesburg, Pretoria, Boksburg, Tsakane and the Hartbeespoort Dam area – renowned for its stunning mountain range and scenic drives.

📇 Stylish Place to Stay

De Hoek Country House, Magaliesburg
One of South Africa's most alluring and accomplished 5 star hotels, De Hoek lies graciously in a serene country setting an hour from Johannesburg and Pretoria. This is an ideal place to stay if you want to explore the Magaliesburg region and get away from it all, but also be close enough to visit Johannesburg for a day trip.

🍽️ Delicious Place to Eat

Goblins Cove Restaurant, Magaliesburg
Venture into the olde world atmosphere of this lovely spot, where faerie's and goblins live and play. The restaurant is quite unique, with its cove shaped architecture, set as it is in a natural forest, on the banks of small lake on the Magaliesburg river.

Opposite from left. Skin, courtesy of
Jennifer Wheatley. Skin, courtesy of
Umberto Adaggi. Below from left.
Still from Hotel Rwanda, courtesy of ZML.
Pool at the Peech Hotel.

Genre: Epics + Historical
Destination: Johannesburg

🎬 Hotel Rwanda (2004)

A historical drama film about the hotelier Paul
Rusesabagina (Don Cheadle) during the Rwandan
Genocide of 1994. The film, which has been
called an African Schindler's List, documents
Rusesabagina's acts to save the lives of his family
and more than a thousand other refugees, by
granting them shelter in the besieged Hôtel des
Mille Collines (which does exist and you can stay
in Kigali). Directed by Terry George, the film was
co-produced by US, British, Italian, and South
African companies, with filming mainly done on
location in Johannesburg, South Africa and some
in Kigali, Rwanda. As an independent film, it had
an initial limited release in theaters, but was
nominated for multiple awards, including Academy
Award nominations for Best Actor, Best Supporting
Actress, and Best Original Screenplay. It continues
to be one of the most–rented films on services,
and is listed by the American Film Institute as one
of the 100 most inspirational movies of all time.

🛏 Stylish Place to Stay

Peech Hotel, Johannesburg
The Peech is a chic boutique hotel. Situated
centrally in Melrose, between Rosebank and
Sandton, it is a swish and sexy hang-out, ideal for
trendy travellers in search of modern luxury. The
Peech Hotel has been described as an 'unexpected
city oasis' and 'contemporary, edgy and Afrocentric'
by leading publications and has been nominated
as Africa's leading Boutique Hotel (World Travel
Awards 2008). It's a real sanctuary.

🍽 Delicious Place to Eat

Moyo, Melrose Arch, Johannesburg
Moyo at Melrose arch, Oozes chi-chi African
charm, this busy chain offers a wide range of
contemporary African eats. Enjoy tastes and
flavours from all over Africa in the heart of modern
Joburg. Relax outside on the square to the soulful
sounds of live African music or cozy up in the
intimate underground dining area built around
natural rock.

Genre: Crime + Gangster
Destination: KwaZulu-Natal

✢ **Regional Information**

KwaZulu Natal has three different geographic areas: the lowland region along the Indian Ocean coast, plains in the central section, and two mountainous areas, the Drakensberg Mountains in the west, and the Lebombo Mountains in the north. The area is a tourist hotspot due to the variety of landscapes and cultural heritage of Zululand, and legacy of the battlefields.

Visiting the battlefields is a must for anyone. Famous military strategists - Shaka, Winston Churchill, Mahatma Gandhi and General Louis Botha - were all part of the KwaZulu-Natal Battlefields. Whilst you can still see small graveyards today, the blood-soaked conflicts live peacefully. Reconciled in this fascinating region are a myriad Battlefield sites, historic towns, national monuments and museums - and in HQs of the British regiments who make a 'pilgrimage' to these fields of bravery and supreme sacrifice.

Zululand is bordered by the Indian Ocean on the east, by Mozambique on the north, and by Swaziland on the west. The Zulus, who belong to the southern branch of the Nguni-speaking peoples, constitute the majority of the population, and Zulu is the chief language. Many Zulus still live as members of a traditional extended family in a fenced compound (kraal), headed by the oldest man, The Zulus became historically important in the early 19th century under Shaka (the chief), whose conquests reduced many neighbouring people to vassalage and caused others to flee. His successors soon encountered the Boer settlers migrating north into Natal as part of the Great Trek (the journey by Afrikaner farmers to flee British domination). This region is a fascinating place to explore, not only due to the historical roots but also the visible cultural heritage that can be seen.

The Drakensberg Mountains or uKhahlamba (the Barrier of Spears) is a 200-kilometre-long mountainous wonderland and world heritage site, and is a particularly popular for travellers who love the outdoors. The Zulu people named it

'uKhahlamba' and the Dutch Voortrekkers 'The Dragon Mountain'. The Drakensberg Mountains, with their awe-inspiring basalt cliffs, snowcapped in winter, tower over riverine bush, lush yellowwood forests and cascading waterfalls, form a massive barrier separating KwaZulu-Natal from the Kingdom of Lesotho. The only road access to the Drakensberg is via Sani Pass, which at the top, boasts the highest pub on Africa, 3,000 metres above sea level.

The uKhahlamba-Drakensberg Park has been preserved since the San people or bushmen roamed these slopes. Tens of thousands of paintings depicting their daily life can be found on the rock faces, and in December 2000, the park received international recognition and was declared KwaZulu-Natal's second World Heritage Site. The fearless may choose to try sheer rock or ice- climbing - or they may prefer the adrenaline rush provided by abseiling, white water rafting or taking a helicopter ride to view the Drakensberg mountains from above.

From Durban to Amanzimtoti, Ballito to Umhlanga Rocks, to the rugged Wild Coast, the highway links popular seaside resorts in rapid succession. The road snakes through subtropical bush, cane fields and hills garlanded with hibiscus blooms. North of Durban, the coastline stretching from the Tugela Mouth to the Umdloti River is aptly known as the Dolphin Coast. Close inshore, shoals of bottle-nose dolphins gambol in the waves.

Arguably the gem of the entire Natal North Coast is the Umhlanga Coastline. The Umhlanga Coastline offers a combination of quiet village life and a cosmopolitan buzz. It also offers a diversity of activities in exotic and magnificent landscapes. Umhlanga, St. Lucia, Mount Edgecombe and Umdloti all nestle alongside one another in a string of first rate beaches and suburbs that not only include a beach of blue flag status, but are collectively some of the most popular beach resort destinations on the east coast of South Africa.

Genre: Crime + Gangster
Destination: KwaZulu-Natal

🎬 Blood Diamond (2006)

Set against the backdrop of civil war and chaos in 1990's Sierra Leone, Danny Archer (played by Leonardo DiCaprio), a South African mercenary, and Solomon Vandy (played by Djimon Hounsou), a fisherman are joined in a common quest to recover a rare pink diamond that can transform their lives. While in prison for smuggling, Archer learns that Solomon - who was taken from his family and forced to work in the diamond fields - has found and hidden the extraordinary rough stone. With the help of Maddy Bowen, an American journalist whose idealism is tempered by a deepening connection with Archer, the two men embark on a trek through rebel territory - a journey that could save Solomon's family and give Archer the second chance he thought he would never have. The film was nominated for five Academy Awards including Best Actor (DiCaprio) and Best Supporting Actor (Hounsou) so was a huge success. Although filming couldn't take place in Sierra Leone, the film does well to encapsulate the realities of the country. Filming actually took place in Kwazulu-Natal, and Cape Town, as well as areas of Maputo in Mozambique.

🛏 Stylish Place to Stay

Thanda Private Game Reserve

Set in the heart of the untamed bush in northern Zululand, Thanda is home to an astonishing variety of wildlife. Thanda means 'love' in Zulu, and there can be no more romantic safari destination; in fact, the private game reserve was voted the World's Leading Luxury Lodge at the 2009 World Travel Awards. Stay in one of the 9 beautifully decorated luxury bush villas overlooking the game reserve or enjoy an even more authentic experience at the non-electrified colonial safari style tented camp.

🍽 Delicious Place to Eat

Thanda Private Game Reserve

The only place to eat if you're staying there, as food is included with the accommodation rates. You won't be disappointed though, as its intimate eating experiences vary from dining out in the bush with candles, to dining under the stars with an excellent world class wine list to boot.

Genre: Crime + Gangster
Destination: KwaZulu-Natal

 ## Zulu (1964)

A historical war film, starring Michael Caine, depicting the Battle of Rorke's Drift between the British Army and the Zulus in January 1879, during the Anglo-Zulu War. Released in 1964, the film has remained popular for over forty years even though film producers and writers were criticised as they tamper with the real-life historical characters. Apparently, several descendants of the soldiers at Rorke's Drift were upset over the portrayal of their relatives in the film.

The location filming couldn't take place at the original site of Rorke's Drift since a modern school and monuments to the battle had been erected over the mission and the battlefield. Besides, from an aesthetic point of view, the scenery wasn't that great. They eventually settled on Drakensberg mountain range about 160km from Rorke's Drift.

Many real Zulus were employed as extras and stunt men. Chief (Then Prince) Buthelezi played the Zulu chief King Cetewayo. He went on to become Minister of Home Affairs in the new South Africa and was even appointed Acting President of the Republic by Nelson Mandela, who had previously been his political rival.

The biggest problem for the director was not arranging the fight scenes but actually getting the Zulus out of the shade - they didn't care much for the sun. The working relationship between the white crew and the Zulus was good and memorable, despite the dark shadow of inhuman apartheid regime. My ship called in at Durban in the late 1960s and we were appalled at the way the blacks were treated. Indeed, Caine vowed never to return to South Africa while apartheid was still in force. Although hundreds of Zulus had worked on the film and appeared in it, because of apartheid they weren't allowed to see it at all: Stanley Baker kept his promise, however, and arranged a secret special viewing for all those involved in the film.

Stylish Place to Stay

Fugitive's Drift, Isandlwana
The spectacular Fugitives' Drift property, a Natural Heritage Site, overlooks both Isandlwana and Rorke's Drift, and includes the site where Lieutenants Melvill and Coghill lost their lives attempting to save the Queen's Colour of their regiment. David and Nicky Rattray, pioneers of heritage tourism in South Africa, created award-winning facilities for visitors to savour the extraordinary saga of the Anglo Zulu War. If one tried to dream up geography and topography for the clash between two great empires, one could hardly come up with a more fantastic scene than these famous battlefields, where the opening battles of the Anglo Zulu war were fought. Our favourite place to stay is the lodge style accommodation with a private veranda overlooking the gorge.

Delicious Place to Eat

Cleopatra Mountain Farmhouse, Drakensburg Mountains
With crystal clear rivers, towering mountains and magnificent scenery, this foodie's paradise is owned and run by Richard and Mouse Poynton. If it's good food you are after- this is the place to be. Cleopatra is fast becoming world-renowned for its innovative menu. The menus change every evening according to the season and availability of local produce. Choose the right bottle of wine from the cellar deep underground.

Genre: Science Fiction
Destination: Soweto

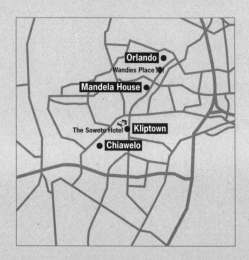

✦ Regional Information

South of Johannesburg is Soweto, a city developed as a township for black people under the apartheid system. Most of the struggle against apartheid was fought in and from Soweto. The name Soweto is an acronym, made up - in apartheid days - from the first letters of the words 'south western township', but some feel it came from the relocating residents asking 'SoWhere To?'

Soweto is inhabited by over two million people, with homes ranging from extravagant mansions to makeshift shacks. Soweto is a city of enterprise and cultural interaction. It is fast becoming a popular tourist destination with sites such as Kliptown (where the Freedom Charter was drawn up), the home of former President Nelson Mandela, the Hector Petersen Memorial site, restaurants and shopping malls – not to mention a recent international films 'Tsotsi' and 'District 9' which has put the city on the map. With several B&B's and restaurants already up and running, the residents of Soweto have found a way to turn a tumultuous history into an income generating tourist attraction.

Soweto is a literally a sprawling township, or more accurately, a cluster of townships on the south-western flank of Johannesburg. Soweto was created in the 1930s, with Orlando the first township established. In the 1950s, more black people were relocated there from 'black spots' in the inner city - black neighbourhoods which the apartheid government had reserved for whites.

Soweto's growth was phenomenal - but unplanned. Despite government attempts to stop the influx of black workers to the cities, waves of migrant workers moved from the countryside and neighbouring countries to look for employment in the city of gold. With a population of over 2 million, the township is the biggest black urban settlement in Africa with a rich political history. Soweto was the centre of political campaigns aimed at the overthrow of the apartheid state. The 1976 student uprising, also known as the Soweto uprising, started in Soweto and spread to the rest of the country. Many of the sights on the heritage route therefore have political significance.

Famous sights are residences of famous anti-apartheid activists. Just a few kilometres drive from Diepkloof, you arrive at Orlando, the first township of Soweto. Here, you can visit Nelson Mandela's first house which is a popular tourist attraction. Mandela stayed here before he was imprisoned in 1961. Security guards will not let you in, but you can see the modest house clearly enough from the street. You can also have a glimpse of the mansion belonging to Winnie Madikizela-Mandela in an affluent part of Orlando West. Archbishop Desmond Tutu's house, the Sisulu residence and the Hector Pieterson memorial museum are in the same neighbourhood. The recently renovated museum offers a detailed account of the events of 1976, including visuals and eye-witness accounts.

Opposite page. Man playing flute, Soweto, courtesy of Dreamstime. **Below from left.** District 9, courtesy of ZML. Kliptown Museum, courtesy of www.joburg.org.za

Genre: Science Fiction
Destination: Soweto

🎬 District 9 (2009)

Strewn with beer bottles, broken glass and giant cacti, this blasted landscape is the stuff of post-apocalyptic science fiction. So perhaps it is no surprise that Chiawelo, a squatter camp in Soweto, is the backdrop to the hit sci-fi blockbuster of the summer 2009.

District 9 is the story of aliens stranded in an impoverished South African township. As their spaceship hovers above Johannesburg the aliens, whose physical appearance earns them the unflattering nickname 'prawns', live in squalid shacks behind barbed wire and barter with gangsters to satisfy their addiction to cat food. The $30m (£18m) film, produced by Lord of the Rings director Peter Jackson, was number one at the US box office in its first weekend and has grossed $90m so far. It has also given the people of Chiawelo an unlikely place in film history. The community, which lacks electricity and running water, gazed in wonder at the arrival of film crew and set-builders at their informal settlement. The spectacle of actors dressed up as aliens caused surprise and even some alarm.

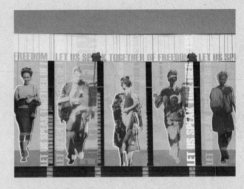

⬐ Stylish Place to Stay

The Soweto Hotel, Soweto
The Soweto Hotel on Freedom Square is located just outside Johannesburg CBD, at the historic national heritage site called the Walter Sisulu Square of Dedication. The Hotel is located adjacent to the Kliptown Museum, showcasing 'the People Shall Govern' exhibition, also dedicated to the events leading to the adoption and signing of the Freedom Charter. Understated elegance sets the tone of this tastefully decorated hotel, themed to the events that are associated with the history of the location. The warm and welcoming face of a younger Nelson Mandela adorn the walls of Reception Desk where guests check-in. The hotel has 46 deluxe standard rooms and 2 Presidential Suites.

🍽 Delicious Place to Eat

Wandie's Place, Soweto
A landmark restaurant in Soweto. A little touristy, but a good place to sample traditional African food: pap (maize paste), bread dumplings, boiled tripe, meaty stews and lots of cold beer. Try the cloudy sorghum beer if you're in an adventurous mood. Probably best to go with a local at night.

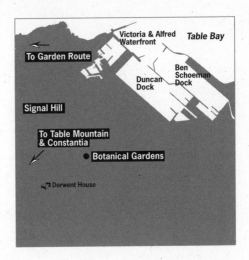

Focus On...
Cape Town

Cape Town is a cosmopolitan city bursting at the seams; with beautiful beaches, glorious vineyards, lush gardens, stylish waterfront and of course fabulous cuisine. It's no wonder that this city is a highlight for many travellers to South Africa, either as a starting point before exploring the Garden Route along the coastline to Port Elizabeth, or as a finish line to relax before heading home. There are plenty of fabulous places to stay from luxury vineyards with spas such as 'The Cellars Hohenort' in Constantia, to boutique downtown gems such as 'Derwent House' in trendy Tamboerskloof.

The highlights of Cape Town are undoubtedly the famous Cape Point, where you can easily cycle along the headland, climb to the top – of if you are feeling less energetic then take the cable car and walk down. The views on a clear day from Table Mountain are incredible; you can see the entire city and some of the townships in the distance, as well as the beautiful coastline. There are various routes to climbing up Table Mountain, whilst you can certainly do this on your own, it pays to have a walking guide with you to show you optional routes and of course points of interest.

Gastronomy is an art that Cape Town has definitely perfected. The sheer variety of seafood, the potion sizes (which 1 plate can feed a family of 4) washed down with fabulous local wine is a dream for foodies. To experience the wonderful vineyards, either in nearby Constantia or Stellenbosch is easily done on your own – although if you are driving you may be limited in terms of tasting, so if you are planning on tasting its best to hire a local guide who can drive for you.

South Africa is a popular destination for international film makers, not least of all because of the reliable weather, unrivalled variety of spectacular locations, stunning scenery and great value for money. Two notable movies in recent years are Ask the dusk (with Colin Farrell) and Lord of War (with Nicholas Cage) these both include many shots of Cape Town and the surrounding area. Other big hit films shot around Cape Town are Catch a Fire (2006), Doomsday (2008) and Oliver Cromwell (2008), as well as independent comedy film 'Cape of Good Hope' (2004) which was entirely filmed in Cape Town at Hout Bay.

ⓘ Stylish Essentials

General Information

General Tourist Information
www.southafrica.net

Johannesburg International Airport
www.worldairportguides.com/johannesburg-jnb

Cape Town International Airport
www.airports.co.za

South African Airways
www.flysaa.com

Etihad Airways
www.etihadairways.com
T. 0800 731 9384 (UK booking line)

Emirates
www.emirates.com/english/
T. 0844 800 2777 (UK booking line)

Baz Bus
www.bazbus.com

Around About Cars
www.aroundaboutcars.com

Avis
www.avis.co.za

Budget
www.budget.co.za

Europcar
www.europcar.co.za

Hertz
www.hertz.co.za

Translux
www.translux.co.za

Greyhound
www.greyhound.co.za

Intercape Mainliner
www.intercape.co.za

SA Roadlink
www.saroadlink.co.za

The Blue Train
www.bluetrain.co.za
T. +27 (12) 334 8459
E. info@bluetrain.co.za

Johannesburg

General Information
www.joburg.org.za

Johannesburg Zoo
www.jhbzoo.org.za
T. +27 (011) 646 2000
E. info@jhbzoo.org.za

Magliesberg Tourist Information
www.magaliesberg.co.za
E. enquiries@magaliesburg.co.za

GoVertical Mountaineering Adventures
Magaliesburg
www.govertical.co.za

Elephant Sanctuary
Hartbeespoort Dam
www.elephantsanctuary.co.za
T. + 27 (12) 258 0332
E. elephantsanctuary@mweb.co.za

Tsakane Safari Camp
www.tsakane.com
E. reservations@tsamanagement.co.za

Lion Park, Johannesburg
www.lion-park.com
E. lionpark@cknet.co.za

De Hoek Country House
www.dehoek.com
T. + 27 (14) 577 9600

Goblins Cove Restaurant
www.goblins.co.za
T. +27 (14) 576 2143
E. goblins@worldonline.co.za

Peech Hotel
www.thepeech.co.za
T. +27 (11) 537 9797
E. reservations@thepeech.co.za

Moyo
Melrose Arch
www.moyo.co.za
T. +27 (11) 684 1477
E. bongi@moyo.co.za
Open: Mon-Sun

KwaZulu-Natal

Tourist Information
www.zulu.org.za

Information on Zululand
www.visitzululand.co.za

Information on Drakensburg
www.drakensberg-tourism.com

Drakensburg Mountain Tours
www.strelitziatours.com
E. info@strelitziatours.com

Tours of Battlefields
www.campaigntrails.co.za

Thanda Private Game Reserve
www.thanda.com
T. + 27 (11) 469-5082
E. reservations@thanda.co.za

Fugitive's Drift
www.fugitives-drift-lodge.com
T.+ 27 (34) 642 1843
E. reservations@fugitivesdrift.com

Cleopatra Mountain Farmhouse
www.cleomountain.com
T. +27 (33) 267 7243
E.cleopatramountain@telkomsa.net

Soweto

Township Tours
www.sowetotour.co.za
E. nik@global.co.za

The Mandela Museum
www.mandelahouse.com
T. +27 (11) 936-7754
E. info@mandelahouse.com
Open: Daily from 9.30–17.00

The Soweto Hotel
www.sowetohotel.co.za
T. +27 (11) 527 7300

Wandie's Place
618 Makhalamele St,
Dube Township
www.wandies.co.za
T. +27 11 982 2796

Cape Town

Stellenbosch Tourist Information
www.tourismstellenbosch.co.za

Constantia Vineyards Information
www.constantiavalley.com
T. +27 (0) 82 332 7844
E. jooles@constantiavalley.com

Cape Point Tourist Information
www.capepoint.co.za
T. +27 (21) 780 9010
E. info@capepoint.co.za

Table Mountain Hiking Guide
www.tablemountainwalks.co.za
T. +27 (21) 7156136
E. mcurran@mweb.co.za

The Cellars Hohenort
www.cellars-hohenort.com
T. +27 21 794 2137
E. reservations@collectionmcgrath.com

Derwent House
www.derwenthouse.co.za
T. +27 21 422 2763
E. reservations@derwenthouse.co.za

Fishing boats, Caribbean, courtesy of Dreamstime.

CARIBBEAN ISLANDS

Bahamas | St. Vincent & the Grenadines |
Puerto Rico | Martinique

U.S.A

● Miami

The Bahamas

North Atlantic Ocean

● Puerto Rico

Caribbean Sea

Martinique ●

St. Vincent & the Grenadines ●

South America

🏆 Why is this place so special?

The Caribbean's stunning beauty helped to attract colonists and explorers to these islands for hundreds of years. The region comprises more than 7,000 islands, islets, reefs, and cays. These islands are actually called the West Indies because when Christopher Columbus landed here in 1492 he believed that he had reached the Indies (in Asia). In more recent times, tourists have flocked here to visit the white beaches, the azure oceans and the stunning scenery, but now the islands are attracting a different kind of traveller: the filmmaker.

The scenery of the Caribbean is now being immortalized on film, and its people have also begun to film on their own, making movies about life in these unique locations. The local film commissions have plenty of reason to portray the islands beauty on film. Film is not only a multi-million dollar industry, and these islands offer a wide variety of unique settings, including exotic nature locations and historic colonial buildings, but being portrayed on film means that tourists travel here in their droves, as they seek out the fabulous locations and to experience the laid back Caribbean life.

While most islands boast being the main setting for at least one or two big movies - a great deal of top movies are shot, at least in part, in the Caribbean. Many of the 'Bond' films have been shot here, perhaps because of the secluded coves and beaches which make great film sets. In the recent remake of the first Bond film, Casino Royale, filmmakers made a return visit to the Bahamas (where scenes for Thunderball, For Your Eyes Only, and The World is Not Enough were filmed) to provide a tropical backdrop for new Bond actor Daniel Craig. Not only did Ian Fleming make his home in Jamaica, but original Bond actor Sean Connery has a home in the Bahamas, on the private housing estate Lyford Cay.

From top. Old San Juan, Puerto Rico, courtesy of Dreamstime. Catamaran in the Grenadines, courtesy of Dreamstime. Colourful Caribbean reef, courtesy of Dreamstime.

Numerous other films that also called in at the Caribbean include Apocalypse Now (Dominican Republic), The Godfather II (Dominican Republic), The Shawshank Redemption (US Virgin Islands), Trading Places (US Virgin Islands), Swiss Family Robinson (Trinidad and Tobago) and the 1999 remake of The Thomas Crown Affair (Martinique).

The Pirates of the Caribbean trilogy have also been synonymous with the Caribbean. They certainly made the most of the region, filming in St. Vincent and the Grenadines, Dominican Republic, The Bahamas, and Bermuda. Hampstead Bay in Dominica was the scene of the waterwheel fight, whilst a small island in the British Virgin Islands appeared as Dead Man's Chest.

Whether you're looking to escape to a secluded beach or wanting to explore some of the incredible coral reefs, the Caribbean islands have a lot to offer independent travellers who don't want to stay in the confines of a holiday resort.

📖 Fast Facts

Capitals: Nassau (Bahamas), Kingstown (St. Vincent and the Grenadines), San Juan (Puerto Rico).

Location: The region is located southeast of the Gulf of Mexico and Northern America, east of Central America, and to the north of South America.

Religion: The largest religious groups in the region are: Christianity, Hinduism, Islam, Rastafari, Santeria, and Voodoo among others.

Languages: Spanish, English, French, Dutch, Haitian Creole and Papiamento are the predominant official languages of various countries in the region, though a handful of unique Creole languages or dialects.

Getting there and exploring around

If you're looking for a quick trip, airplane travel is your best bet. Numerous major airline carriers - from departure points all over the world - have regular flights to the Caribbean. If you are flying from the UK though, it is likely you'll have to fly via the United States, such as Miami, and sometimes the indirect routes are often the cheapest. Although, some airlines such as British Airways and Virgin Atlantic do offer direct routes from both London and Manchester to Bahamas, Barbados and Puerto Rico.

Most flights from the United States are nonstop to the Caribbean, and direct flights typically connect in San Juan or St. Thomas. A word on airline lingo: a nonstop flight does not make any stops, but a direct flight may make at least one stop along the way. If you are planning a longer extended trip, then it may make sense to buy an air pass with Star Alliance, which will allow you the flexibility to extend your trip to the USA, Central America and Caribbean.

Once you're in the Caribbean, you can island hop by way of one of the many small Caribbean airlines, such as Air Charter Bahamas, American Eagle, Air Martinique, Bahamasair, Winward Island airways, Liat airlines also offers hopping passes from Puerto Rico to St Vincent and Dominica. BWIA also offers a Caribbean air pass, for up to 30 days you may travel to an extensive list of island destinations throughout the Caribbean for an all-inclusive price of $399. Island Hopper from Air Jamaica is the newest pass in the region and is a great bargain for extensive travel.

Better yet, chart your own boat. Charter a private 'bareboat' and sail through the crystal blue Caribbean waters at your own pace just as Sir Francis Drake did; hire a skippered boat for a little company, or embark on a fully crewed yacht for total luxury on the high seas. Crewed yachts come complete with a personal chef and an expert captain, so all you have to do is relax. Alternatively if you are a diving enthusiast, then one of the best ways of exploring hidden reefs is by live-aboard. These can be as luxurious as you want, usually a live-aboard trip lasting 10 days will allow you ample time to explore the excellent reefs, and stop off at some of the islands too.

Best time of year to visit

The high season for tourism in the Caribbean is winter, which is typically mid-December to mid-April. This is the time of year that usually has the driest weather in the Caribbean, and the coldest weather in the Northern U.S. and Canada.

Hotels charge their highest prices during this peak season, and reservations will have to be made well in advance. Christmas, and spring break is especially popular, so plan many months ahead if you'd like to spend the holidays in the Caribbean. February is also a peak time, especially around the weekend of President's Day in the United States.

The off-season–mid-April to mid-December–means reduced rates. Many hotels offer rooms at a 20 to 50 percent reduction during this time, so summer travel to the Caribbean can be quite appealing. In addition to saving money during the off-season, you'll enjoy less crowded beaches, streets and shops.

Hurricane season, from mid-April through mid-December, should not necessarily be ruled out. Even if a hurricane hits somewhere in the region, any single island's mainland may only feel the effects in the form of heavy rains. Be sure to check the forecast, though; if it's all clear, look for deeply discounted packages during this time.

Do be aware, however, that the sun shines brighter during these months and some restaurants and stores only open during the peak season. Some Caribbean hotels may use the off-season to do renovations and construction, but proper research can help you find adequate facilities.

December in the Bahamas is a fabulous time, due to the Junkanoo street festival (a Bahamian festival that occurs during the dark hours of morning on the 26th of December and again bringing in its first hours of light on the first day of the new year), and of course the annual Bahamian International Film festival, which again is every December.

? Must know before you go

Small airports. Most Caribbean airports are small, so arriving passengers cannot typically deplane directly to the terminal. Few airports provide shuttle service, so expect a long walk on the tarmac to the terminal to claim your luggage.

Check-in security. Due to increased terrorist activity in recent years, airports have enhanced security measures, especially in the U.S. In addition to regular baggage screening procedures, airports now have additional required security checks. Many airports also conduct random passenger inspections at which point security personnel conduct a complete search of the person and all of all their belongings. Because of these added security stops, you should plan on arriving at the airport so you have ample time to pass through all of the security clearance points.

Watch out for extras. When budgeting your accommodation costs, remember that most hotels in the Caribbean will add a government tax (currently averaging about 7.5%) and a service charge (currently averaging about 10 to 15%), to your final bill that will not necessarily have been part of your quoted price.

Highlights

Dive in style. Dive the crystal clear waters in the Exuma Cays, Bahamas.

Explore colonial culture. Visit the oldest and best preserved colonial city in the Americas, San Juan, Puerto Rico.

Sail along. Charter a private yacht and sail around Tobago Cays, Grenadines.

Laze on a beach. The beauty and the incredible diversity of the Martinique beaches are simply amazing

Star Spotting

Bump into one of the many celebrity residents of the Bahamas at Lyford Cay (where Sean Connery owns a property) or the Exumas where Johnny Depp is said to own an island.

Genre: Action + Adventure
Destination: Bahamas

⚓ Regional Information

With 700 islands, 2,500 cays and 500 miles of the clearest water in the world, the Bahamas is said to have it all: glorious beaches, warm surf, fabulous coral reefs, and challenging golf courses. The most popular destination is Nassau/Paradise Island, just 35 minutes by air from Miami. On the outer Islands (The Abacos, Eleuthera/Harbour Island, Long Island, Cat Island and The Exumas) you'll find pristine diving and fishing sites, coupled with a more authentic West Indian character.

Tourists and expats have been flocking to the Bahamas for decades, and whilst the islands do boast a celebrity following, no-one can quite deny the effect that the film industry has had on tourism. Bond in particular has become synonymous with the Bahamas. In 1965, Sean Connery starred in Thunderball—the fourth episode of Ian Fleming's 007 series—an action-packed movie shot mostly underwater and on the Bahamian island of New Providence. The film's classic moments firmly established the old colonial capital, Nassau, and the beaches of offshore Paradise Island, as the getaway for the jet set: the sight of James Bond dining in a pink linen shirt at the waterfront restaurant Café Martinique, playing baccarat in a black-tie Nassau casino, and diving through coral reefs in a red wet suit proved irresistible. Shaken and stirred, pleasure-seekers began flocking to the white sands and martini-clear waters: by 1968, this 700-island archipelago had more than a million visitors a year. The Bahamas is firmly on the tourist map, but hasn't lost credibility and appeal for filmmakers, and has now established its own International Film Festival, which runs annually in December.

James Bond fans can enjoy themselves spotting scenes from their favourite Bond flicks. Nassau Harbour was used for many of the underwater battle scenes, as well as being the hiding place of the stolen Vulcan bomber, in Thunderball. If you're into diving, you can visit the Tears of Allah shipwreck in the South Ocean which featured in Never Say Never Again. Casinos have also played a huge role in many Bond films; and

here there are plenty of glitzy and glamorous ones, like Wyndham Nassau Resort & Crystal Palace Casino and Atlantis Paradise Island Resort & Casino. If you are looking for something more relaxed then head to homier bars like Ronnie's Smoke Shop & Sports Bar on Eleuthera and Palms at Three Sisters in George Town, Grand Exuma. You'll also find plenty of clubs offering music and dancing throughout the islands. The Bahamas is also well known for its special event 'Junkanoo', a musical street parade comparable to New Orleans' Mardi Gras. It is held on Boxing Day (December 26th) and New Year's Day and features bright, colourful costumes and irresistibly rhythmic music produced by cowbells, drums and brass horns. It's a fabulous time of year to visit, as the streets are full with atmosphere.

Other films shot on location in the Bahamas include Cocoon, Jaws IV: The Revenge and Speed 2: Cruise Control. South Bimini Island, around 40 miles east of Miami, has also made a film appearance, albeit very briefly, at the end of Silence of the Lambs when Hannibal (Anthony Hopkins) calls Clarice (Jodie Foster) to tell he's 'having an old friend for dinner' before walking down King's Highway in Bimini.

The crystal waters and sandy beaches of the Bahamas are a constant draw for film makers. Bahamian beaches are incredibly varied. Six-mile long Cable Beach on New Providence Island is lined by shops, casinos, restaurants, bars, and water-sports operators. Cabbage Beach on Paradise Island is flanked by mega-resorts and can be crowded. Those seeking solitude head to Treasure Cay in the Abacos, a stunning, almost empty, 3.5 mile flour-white strip. Gold Rock Beach is part of Lucayan National Park, a protected area that contains some of Grand Bahama's wildest, most secluded, and gorgeous beaches. The best way to explore the secluded beaches is without a doubt by boat, or better still take a live-aboard boat for a week if you plan to do some diving.

Genre: Action + Adventure
Destination: Bahamas

🎬 After the Sunset (2004)

The plot centered around two master thieves, Max Burdett (Brosnan) and his beautiful accomplice Lola, (Hayek) who are finally retiring. Fresh from their final score – and with their financial future set – the couple has come to Paradise Island in the Bahamas to relax and enjoy their hard-earned riches, but Stan (an FBI agent played by Harrelson) refuses to believe it. The film was almost entirely shot in the Bahamas. Director Brett Ratner admits "The Bahamas offered all the great temptations: casinos, beautiful women, and cheap Rolexes." But the director insists he set After the Sunset here more for the island's aesthetic advantages than for its abundant luxuries. "The colour, the quality of light and water, the music, and the friendly vibe stimulated my senses," he says. Much of the film, which coincidentally stars 007 veteran, Pierce Brosnan, unfolds at Atlantis, the Vegas-style, aquatic-themed resort on Paradise Island. It also takes in many of Nassau's sights and sounds, following the duo aboard a cruise ship in the harbour, through a festive street parade, and into the city square for a sultry samba. With its intoxicating blend of romance, action, and comedy, After the Sunset has lured a new generation of travellers.

🛏 Stylish Place to Stay

Kamalame Cay, Andros Islands

The Andros Islands are one of those rare Caribbean gems that are still largely unexplored and sparsely populated. Kamalame is a perfect island hideaway with a touch of luxury. The beachfront cottage suites are sumptuous and spacious villa suites are with lofted ceilings and French doors opening to sun-swept verandas — it's a perfect nesting place. It also has an over water spa recently which recently opened.

🍽 Delicious Place to Eat

Graycliffe, Nassau

One of the top dining spots is Graycliff's restaurant — considered one of the finest in the Caribbean — so it's not surprising that stars like Nicolas Cage, Michael Jordan and Brooke Shields have eaten here. Its exquisite creations include Bahamian lobster in a cream sauce and sautéed grouper on a bed of spinach with a mustard sauce, while the wine cellar boasts more than 175,000 bottles.

Genre: Action + Adventure
Destination: Bahamas

Casino Royale (2006)

Both New Providence Island (where Nassau is located) and Paradise Island play major roles in the 2006 remake of Casino Royale, starring Daniel Craig as the new James Bond. Nassau's Albany House plays the role of a beach villa owned by the villain Dimitrios and Bond's future girlfriend, Solange. The Buena Vista Hotel and Restaurant stands in for the Madagascar Embassy in the film. Major scenes for Casino Royale also were shot at the Atlantis resort and the neighbouring One&Only Ocean Club on Paradise Island. In fact, you'll get a pretty good look at the Ocean Club's beautiful lobby and a beachfront villa in some of the movie's early scenes, and of the beach scene with Craig emerging from the ocean in his trunks. Other scenes were shot at Coral Harbour and Nassau International Airport. You may also be surprised to discover that the interior of Miami International Airport was actually Nassau International Airport, whilst the Madagascar shanty town was filmed at an abandoned motel in Coral Harbour on New Providence Island.

Stylish Place to Stay

One & Only Ocean Club, Nassau

Stylish and suave, just like Bond. This once private hideaway of A&P heir Huntington Hartford, this ultra expensive resort on magnificent Cabbage Beach's quietest stretch provides the ultimate in understated —and decidedly posh—elegance. The Versailles gardens include 35 acres of terraced serenity and an imported French cloister. Set amid private gardens, the spacious colonial-style rooms have intricately carved furniture, marble bathrooms, and private butlers. The open-air restaurant, Dune, is perched over the beach.

Delicious Place to Eat

Café Matisse, Nassau

Set directly behind Parliament House, in a mustard-beige-coloured building built a century ago as a private home, this restaurant is on everybody's short list of downtown Nassau favourites. It serves well-prepared Italian and international cuisine in a setting decorated with colourful Matisse prints. It's run by the sophisticated Bahamian-Italian team Greg and Gabriella Curry, who prepare menu items that include calamari with spicy chili-flavoured jam, served with tomatoes and fresh mozzarella cheese; a mixed grill of seafood; grilled filet of local grouper served with a light tomato-caper sauce; spaghetti with lobster; grilled rack of lamb with gravy; a perfect filet mignon in a green-peppercorn sauce; and a zesty curried shrimp with rice.

Genre: Romantic Comedy
Destination: St. Vincent & the Grenadines

✈ Regional Information

St Vincent and the Grenadines may conjure up all kinds of visions of exotic, idyllic island life. Imagine an island chain buried deep within the Caribbean Sea, uncluttered by tourist exploitation. Thirty-two islands dot the seascape, all vying to one-up each other in terms of tranquility. St Vincent is the largest in the group, home to the capital, Kingstown, which is a lively town and a throwback to colonial times with cobblestone streets and locals rushing about. Once you get off the beaten track, everything changes. Gone is the traffic, the hustle and the pavements. All you're left with is a smattering of tiny islands waiting to be explored. In Bequia, secluded beaches stretch out before you, the pace of life slows to a crawl and the desire to go home vanishes. You'll find unassuming budget hideaways, where you can escape from the world. Or you can spend time on the island of Mustique, a hideaway for the rich and famous, where renting a house for the week will cost more than buying a luxury car.

These islands were once the realm of real pirates but now they are the stomping grounds of the film series 'Pirates of the Caribbean'. St Vincent and the Grenadines really jumped into the limelight thanks to Hollywood and they're not looking back. Travellers here can feed their taste for adventure - as well as seclusion - by visiting sites used in the movie series and exploring some of the Caribbean's most protected bays both above and below the waves. The movie is historically grounded in fact, as St. Vincent was no stranger to pirates who stumbled upon a last stronghold of the Carib Indians against the onslaught of French and English colonisers. Today's more peaceful buccaneers will find in St. Vincent a last bastion of a Caribbean that pre-dates the era of mass tourism.

St. Vincent's capital Kingstown on the south-western coast is a vibrant town of 18th century architecture. Visit the lively produce market (open Mondays - Saturdays) or 'church-hop' through the island's rich history from St. George Cathedral (built 1820) and Cathedral of the Assumption (1823) to Kingstown Methodist (1841) and Scots Kirk (1880).

The islands have also enchanted sailors for centuries, and continue to do so. Whether you have your own vessel or are happy to hitch a ride, the island-hopping opportunities are irresistible. Yachting is very much part of the life here; with sailing hotspots dotted everywhere, and places like Tobago Cays are considered by some as the best in the world. Tobago Cays are really exceptional, and they now form a marine park, protected by a big horseshoe-shaped coral reef and four small islands (Petit Rameau, Petit Bateau, Baradal and Jamesby). Opposite, on the other side of the reef, is Petit Tabac Island, where 'Pirates of the Caribbean' was filmed. This is where Jack Sparrow was held prisoner and escaped by tying two turtles together. There are plenty of turtles in the Tobago Cays, as well as beautiful seabeds along the horseshoe-shaped reef, which makes diving a dream. But if you feel you have the soul of a real 'Crusoe', and enjoy deserted anchorages, you must go to 'World's End reef'. The entry is quite easy and the reefs easily visible, its deserted anchorage in the middle of nowhere, means you can experience some extraordinary diving. Be aware, however, that this is only a daytime anchorage; staying overnight could be risky. Another place not to be missed is the anchorage at Windward Bay, on Mayreau Island. This deserted anchorage, just opposite the Tobago Cays, is where you can spend the night with no problems, as long as you don't bump into any pirates of course!

Finally a trip here wouldn't be complete without visiting Bequia, the largest of the 32 islands. Its boat-building, whaling and fishing heritage is alive in the craftsmanship of model boat makers who sell their wares along the beaches - and will hand-fit anything from a traditional wooden schooner to a custom-made replica of almost any yacht. There are 35 stunning dives sites in and around Bequia including 'The Bullet' where rays, barracuda and nurse sharks mingle; 'Devil's Table' for a chance to float above a sunken sailboat wreck; and the 90-foot drop aptly named 'The Wall.' You can hop here for a half day by taking the local ferry from Kingstown, or stay for longer at one of the local inns.

Genre: Romantic Comedy
Destination: St. Vincent & the Grenadines

🎬 Pirates of the Caribbean: film series (2003, 2006, 2007)

A cult series directed by Gore Verbinski, based on a Walt Disney theme park ride of the same name, follow Captain Jack Sparrow (Johnny Depp), Will Turner (Orlando Bloom), and Elizabeth Swann (Keira Knightley). The trilogy was first released in 2003 with Pirates of the Caribbean: The Curse of the Black Pearl. After the unexpected success of this, Walt Disney Pictures revealed that a trilogy was in the works. Pirates of the Caribbean: Dead Man's Chest, was released three years later on July 7, 2006. The sequel proved to be very successful, breaking records worldwide the day of its premiere. The last film in the trilogy, Pirates of the Caribbean: At World's End was released worldwide in 2007, totalling $2.79 billion worldwide in film franchise. In September 2008, Depp signed on for a fourth film, Pirates of the Caribbean: On Stranger Tides, expected to be released in Summer 2011. The Curse of the Black Pearl made use of the pristine beaches of the Winward islands, the capital Kingstown, the waters around Bequia, and Walillabou Bay, where the 'Port Royal' set was built - the facade still remain; and Chateaubelair, where a town and cave-like set (now torn down) went up for the movie.

🛏 Stylish Place to Stay

Firefly Plantation, Bequia
Firefly Plantation is built on the estate of an 18th century West Indian homestead, now a 30 acre working plantation with hillsides of orchards producing oranges, grapefruit, bananas, breadfruit, guava, Bequia plums and mangos. Firefly has its own unique character and charm, friendly attentive staff, excellent food and cocktails. The 4 beautifully appointed guest rooms are located in a separate building within the grounds with wonderful views across the plantation coconut groves and over the bay. This place is a real barefoot, chic retreat.

🍽 Delicious Place to Eat

The Bounty Restaurant, Kingstown
Captain Bligh of the HMS Bounty brought the first breadfruit tree to the island to feed slaves - and direct descendents of this tree abound here. Stay in character by enjoying West Indian food at The Bounty restaurant, whose daily menu reflects the produce and catch of the day. Great place for a spot of lunch, while exploring the town.

Genre: Science Fiction
Destination: Puerto Rico

Puerto Rico is 100 long by 35 miles wide and as a result of its geographical position in the centre of the arc of the Antilles, Puerto Rico is essentially a crossroads of Hispanic and Anglo cultures. Despite it's very diverse influx of cultures, Puerto Rico has been a part of the United States since 1898 and Puerto Ricans have been U.S. citizens since 1917. Close to 4 million people live on the 'Island of Enchantment,' with more than a million in the greater San Juan metropolitan area alone. It is a vibrant, modern, bilingual, multicultural society, one that has been molded by Spanish, African, Indian and U.S. influences. Residents of Puerto Rico have much in common with their fellow Americans in the continental United States, yet they retain a decidedly Hispanic heritage.

Perhaps because of its status as a U.S. Commonwealth, Puerto Rico's film history stretches back to the days of silent movies. Although the first films to shoot there were U.S. productions, the local movie industry is well-established, too. Aside from its locations, Puerto Rico appeals to filmmakers because its experienced crew members and eager film commission make shooting here a pleasure. Of course, its 40 percent tax break for film productions also serves as a huge incentive. Local productions have also been boosted by financial incentives, loans, and grants.

One of the earliest films to feature local actors, Maruja (1959), depicted life in Puerto Rico at the time. The movie rocketed its stars to fame. Many of them went on to highly successful careers on Puerto Rican television programs. From the campy Frankenstein Meets the Spacemonster (1965), in which Martians land on Puerto Rico and kidnap go-go dancers, to Steven Spielberg's Oscar-nominated Amistad (1997), every type of movie you can imagine has been made here. Though, it has been popular for 'science fiction' films such as Contact (1997) and 'Lord of the Flies' (1963).

For any traveller coming to Puerto a visit to the city's capital San Juan is a must. Established in 1521, San Juan is the second-oldest European-founded settlement in the

Americas (after Santo Domingo) and the oldest under US jurisdiction. If you are interested in history, enjoy a walk on the ramparts, where half a millennium ago Spanish soldiers held their watch. Begin your journey with three stunning Spanish Colonial Fortresses: El Morro, Fuerte San Cristóbal and La Fortaleza, designated as World Heritage Sites by UNESCO. Visiting Old San Juan, is magnificent. The walled city, with it's rounded with magical architecture, churches and chapels, fountains, statues and plazas where you can relax with a locally brewed coffee and watch the world go by.

Puerto Rico's Arecibo Observatory, the world largest and most sensitive telescope, located about 10 miles south of the town of Arecibo, has featured in several films. The huge radio telescope was used by Jodie Foster in Contact to probe the cosmos, it appeared as the Cuban satellite dish in Goldeneye and it also received transmissions from an alien source in Species, which makes it a bit of a tourist hotspot for those who like astronomy, and all things UFO related. It's not quite as pristine as it looks in the movie and had to be cleaned up with a little computer generated help. It's operated by Cornell University, and if you want to visit, there is a visitor centre.

The California of Puerto Rico is Rincon, known as 'Pueblo del Surfing' (the surfing town) and 'El Pueblo de los Bellos Atardeceres' (the town of beautiful sunsets). Located in the Western Coastal Valley, west of Añasco and Aguadilla, it boasts big surf breaks and dudes cool enough to chill a box of beer. The half-dozen reef-lined Atlantic beaches have become a winter mecca for skilled surfers since the World Surfing Championship was held here nearly twenty years ago. There are a few surf schools that offer surfing lessons for different levels, and a surf camp where you can learn to surf in an intensive setting. Endangered humpback whales visit in the winter, so visiting here any time of year is a travellers dream.

Further afield is the island of Vieques which travel experts around the world are calling the island the next 'hottest Caribbean destination' located just 6 miles off the southeast coast of Puerto Ricoand reachable by ferry or boat. Since the U.S. Navy's departure in 2003, Isla de Vieques has seen an increase on the number of tourists and many changes have already taken place, with little hotels popping up everywhere. Vieques has also been used as a film location, most notably for 'Heartbreak Ridge' (starring Clint Eastwood who also directed the film) and the 'Lord of the Flies' (1963). One of the most fascinating things to do is spend a few hours day kayaking the clear waters, coupled with swimming with sea turtles makes the island attractive to nature lovers.

Even further afield is the island of Culebra. The mainland's weird, wonderful and distinctly wacky smaller cousin that lies glistening like a bejewelled Eden to the east. Long feted for its diamond dust beaches and world-class diving reefs, sleepy Culebra is probably more famous for what it hasn't got than for what it actually possesses. There are no big hotels here, no golf courses, no casinos, no fast-food chains, no rush-hour traffic and no post modern stress. Situated 17 miles to the east of the mainland, but inhabiting an entirely different planet culturally speaking, the island's peculiar brand of off-beat charm can sometimes take a bit of getting used to. There's but one binding thread – the place is jaw-droppingly beautiful. There are only 3 known films which used Culebra as a setting, these were Cayo (2005), Culebra (1971) and The Frogmen (1951), we doubt it will be long before a major film production companies steal this island for screen.

Genre: Science Fiction
Destination: Puerto Rico

Contact (1997)

The story features the rational scientist Dr Ellie Arroway (Jodie Foster) who is the recipient of apparent alien messages in this interesting, adaptation of Carl Sagan's novel. She and her colleagues listen to radio transmissions in hopes of finding signals sent by extraterrestrial life. Government scientist David Drumlin pulls the funding from SETI. After eighteen months of searching, Ellie gains funding from reclusive billionaire industrialist S.R. Hadden, which allows her to continue her studies at the Very Large Array in New Mexico. The film was released on July 1, 1997 to mixed reviews. Although the film did win the Hugo Award for Best Dramatic Presentation and received multiple awards and nominations at the Saturn Awards. The release of Contact was publicized by controversies from the Bill Clinton Administration, CNN, as well as individual lawsuits from George Miller and Francis Ford Coppola. Filmed in several locations across the USA (such as Mojave Desert, California, Hotel Washington in Washington DC, but mainly set in Puerto Rico's Arecibo, Arecibo Observatory, and Ciales.

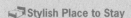 Stylish Place to Stay

Hotel Casa Grande, Utuado
Set in a stunning valley on 107 lush tropical Cuerdas less than two hours from San Juan, Casa Grande Mountain Retreat is an oasis of peace and tranquillity. The former coffee plantation, now exquisitely landscaped, has 20 rooms scattered up the mountainside, each with private bath, balcony, and hammock. While there are no TVs or phones in any of the rooms, there are daily yoga classes, a scrumptious on-site restaurant and every available excuse to sit around all day and do – absolutely nothing.

Delicious Place to Eat

La Mallorquina, San Juan
What better place to enjoy an authentic Puerto Rican meal than at the city's oldest restaurant? Established in 1848 this spot has been lovingly run by the Rojos family since 1900. The house special is 'asopao', a thick stew made with rice and chicken, lobster or shrimp. Sample fresh gazpacho for a starter and save room for some coconut flan or a Pina Colada.

Genre: Science Fiction
Destination: Puerto Rico

🎬 Lord of the Flies (1963)

'Lord of the Flies' is a classic 1963 film adaptation of William Golding's novel of the same name. It was directed by the renowned theatre director Peter Brook and produced by Lewis M. Allen, known since for producing films based on modern-classic novels. The film was in production for much of 1961 though the film was not released until 1963. Golding himself supported the film. When Kenneth Tynan was a script editor for Ealing Studios he commissioned a script of 'Lord of the Flies' from Nigel Kneale, but Ealing Studios closed in 1959 before it could be produced. The film was filmed entirely in Puerto Rico at Aguadilla, El Yunque and on the island of Vieques. Apparently, during the first week of film shooting on the Island of Vieques, Puerto Rico, the Bay of Pigs Invasion began. This impacted filming because the wounded were evacuated to the U.S. naval hospital on Vieques.

🛏 Stylish Place to Stay

Hix Island House, Vieques
Eco-chic house, nestled into the hillside and set in a 13-acre natural refuge of native trees, tall grasses, birds and butterflies. Yet with all the comforts you need, such as Frette bathrobes, in room massage, daily yoga classes, and on site gourmet provisions such as homemade bread, local fruit juices and Puerto Rican coffee. Our favourite room is loft 3, the adobe.

🍽 Delicious Place to Eat

Café Coconuts, Vieques
This is the place everyone goes for breakfast - just a simple little place with a few tables - decent food fast and service with a smile. Located in the heart of town near the ferry. Good place to sit, have a drink and relax while looking around town.

Opposite page from top. Old Barrels.
Trabaud Beach, Martinique. Both courtesy
of Dreamstime.

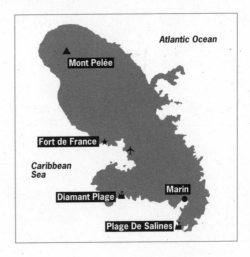

Focus On...
Martinique

The sights and sounds of Martinique have long been attracting tourists from all over the world. From the mountainous northern region down to the stunning south coast and in between, Martinique tourism thrives as thousands of visitors arrive each year, with its historic plantations, museums, scenic natural areas, and bustling towns and cities all add to the island's appeal. It's no wonder that filmmakers of the Thomas Crown Affair (1999) chose this island. The clever drama remake featuring Pierce Brosnan, as the wealthy and adventurous playboy businessman who savors a good challenge, and steals a priceless Monet from the New York City Metropolitan Museum of Art; was almost entirely filmed in Martinique. The house used as Crown's Caribbean get-away is owned by one of the 30 original families who settled in Martinique in the 1600s, but the interior and the scenes around it, like the beach, are a montage of various other parts of Martinique and sound stages constructions.

Beach lovers have plenty of choices from the relative solitude of 'Diamont' and 'Plage des Salines' to the 'see and be seen' spots that are 'Pointe du Bout' and 'Pointe de Marin'. One of the island's more unique treasures, though, is situated north of St-Pierre, where the black sand 'Anse Céron' which affords spectacular sunsets and world class snorkelling

The large collection of plantation houses and historic estates around the island are particularly appealing to those who admire unique architecture and abundant history, Clement House, or Habitation Clement, is only one of the many Martinique sights offering a photo gallery of prominent musicians, politicians, and artists that were past guests, shaded walks around the property and a rum factory right on the grounds where samples are poured freely.

Martinique attractions definitely include the many events that take place throughout the year. From famous Carnival to the Martinique Jazz Festival to boat races and music festivals, there's literally something happening in every month of the year. Be sure to check the calendar of events before a visit to secure accommodation and avoid disappointment.

Martinique tourism is heavy around the famous site of the eruption of 1902 at Mount Pelee. Literally wiping out the town and residents of St Pierre in minutes, the famous natural disaster has left remnants of the old town of St Pierre well below it while the new town of St Pierre grows and thrives around the ruins. Head to the top of the mountain for scenic views and tour the ruins for a good look into a paramount era in the island's past.

Known for a degree of excellence in island rum, distillery tours are as popular as the beaches and shopping in Martinique. The rum industry relies heavily on both Martinique tourism as well as export of the world-class liquor. Rum distillery tours are available to the public where the end is normally marked by a satisfying and complimentary rum tasting. Famous island distilleries include St-James, Million Distilleries Plantation, and Trois Rivières.

ⓘ Stylish Essentials

General Information

General Tourist Information
www.caribbeantravel.com

Air Charter Bahamas
www.aircharterbahamas.com

American Eagle
www.aa.com
T. +1 800 433 7300
(US reservations line)

Air Caraïbes
www.aircaraibes-usa.com

Bahamasair
www.bahamasair.com
T. +1 242 377 5505
(Local reservations line)

British Airways
www.ba.com
T. 0844 493 0 787
(UK reservations line)

**Caribbean Airlines
(formally BWIA)**
www.caribbean-airlines.com
T. 0870 774 7336
(UK reservations line)
E. mail@caribbean-airlines.com

Liat Airlines
www.liatairline.com
T. +1 268 480 5601
(Local reservations)
E. reservations@liatairline.com

Virgin Atlantic
www.virgin-atlantic.com
T. 0844 874 7747
(UK reservations line)

Windward Island Airways
www.fly-winair.com
T. +1 599 5454237
E. reservations@fly-winair.com

Live-aboard Companies in the Caribbean

Explorer Adventures in Bahamas
St Kitts, Grenadines
www.explorerventures.com
E. info@explorerventures.com

The Agressor Fleet
www.aggressor.com
T. +1 985 385 2628
E. info@aggressor.com

Peter Hughs Liveaboards
www.peterhughes.com
T. +1 800 932 6237
E. dancer@peterhughes.com

Private Skippered yachts/boats

Caribbean Yacht charter
www.sailingdirections.com
E. info@sailingdirections.com

Caribbean Sail
www.caribbeansail.com
T. +1 (268) 463 7101
E. charters@caribbeansail.com

Bahamas

General Tourist Information
www.bahamas.co.uk
T. +44 (0) 20 7355 0800
E. info@bahamas.co.uk

**Bahamas International
Film festival**
www.bintlfilmfest.com

Junkanoo Festival
www.junkanoo.com

Diving in Bahamas

Stuart's Cove Dive Centre
www.stuartcove.com
E. info@stuartcove.com

Exuma Watersports Tour
Exuma Cays sightseeing and
Snorkelling Safari
www.exumawatersports.com
T. +1 242 336 3422

Diving in the Exumas
www.dive-exuma.com
T. +1 242 336 2893
E. diveexuma@hotmail.com

One & Only Ocean Club
www.oneandonlyresorts.com
T. +1 242 363 2501
E. reservations@oneandonlyresorts.com

Café Matisse
Bank Lane, Nassau,
New Providence Island
T. +1 242 356 7012
Open: Tues-Sat 12.00–15.00
and 18.00–22.00

Kamalame Cay
www.kamalame.com
T. +1 876 632 3213 (reservations)
E. info@kamalame.com

Graycliffe's Restaurant
www.graycliff.com
T. +1 242 302 9150
Open: 12.00–15.00 and
18.30–22.00

St. Vincent & the Grenadines

Government website
www.gov.vc

General Tourist Information
www.discoversvg.com

Tobago Cays Information
www.tobagocays.com

Bequia Information
www.bequia-information.com

Yacht charter company
www.barefootyachts.com
T. +1 784 456 9526
E. barebum@vincysurf.com

Sailing company
www.FriendshipRose.com
T. +1 784 495 0886
E. friendshiprose@mac.com

Bequia diving
www.bequiaDiveAdventures.com
T. +1 784 458 3826
E. Adventures@vincysurf.com

Day tours of Tobago Cays
www.fantaseatours.com
T. +1 784 457 4477
E. fantasea@vincysurf.com

Bequia Ferry Express
www.bequiaexpress.net
T.+ 1 784 458 3472

Firefly Plantation, Bequia
www.fireflybequia.com
T. +1 784 458 3414
E. stan@fireflybequia.com

Bounty restaurant
Egmont St., Kingstown,
T. +1 784 456 1776

Puerto Rico

General Tourist Information
www.gotopuertorico.com

Arecibo Observatory
www.naic.edu

Blue Caribe Kayaks, Vieques
www.enchanted-isle.com/bluecaribe
T. +1 787 741 2522

Surfing school, Rincon
www.surfandboard.com
T. +1 787 823 0610
E. surfsup@coqui.net

Vieques Tourist Information
www.viequestravelguide.com

Hotel Casa Grande
www.hotelcasagrande.com
T. +1 787 894 3939
E. tarzan@hughes.net

La Mallorquina
Calle San Justo 207, San Juan
T.+1 787 722 3261
Open: Daily 11.30–22.00

Hix Island House
www.hixislandhouse.com
T. + 1 787 741 2302
E. info@hixislandhouse.com

Café Coconuts
Downtown Isabel Segunda, Vieques
www.coconutsvieques.com
T. +1 787 741 9325
Open: Tues-Sun 07.30 till lunch

Martinique

General Tourist Information
www.martinique.org

Mount Pelee
www.mount-pelee.com

Clement House
www.habitation-clement.fr
T. +1 0596 54 62 07

Rum Distilleries

Saint-James & Rum Museum
Le Bourg, Sainte-Marie
Open: daily from 9.00–17.00

La Mauny Distillery
Riviere Pilote
www.rhumdemartinique.com
Open: 9.00–17.30

Dillon Distillery
Route de Chateauboef,
Fort de France
www.rhums-dillon.com
Open: 9.00–16.00

Trois Rivières
Saint-Luce
www.plantationtroisrivieres.com
Open: 9.00–17.30

Snake charmer, courtesy of Dreamstime.

INDIA

Rajasthan | Delhi | Karnataka | Mumbai

🏆 Why is this place so special?

Since India got its independence from Britain in 1947 after a long struggle led mostly by Mahatma Gandhi., it has made huge progress and coped with great problems. It has developed its industry, its agriculture, and has maintained a system of government which makes it the largest democracy in the world. India is a perfect 'independent travellers' destination, and not just for the intrepid backpacker, but also the 'luxury backpacker', abundant with heritage sites, rich in culture, glorious beaches, wellness spas, the great outdoors, not to mention every type of accommodation from chic retreats, to luxurious palaces.

India is set apart from the rest of Asia by the Himalayas, the highest, youngest and still evolving mountain chain on the planet. India holds virtually every kind of landscape imaginable. An abundance of mountain ranges and national parks provide ample opportunity for eco-tourism and trekking, and its sheer size promises something for everyone. North India is the country's largest region, and begins with Jammu and Kashmir, with terrain varying from arid mountains in the far north to the lake country and forests near Srinagar and Jammu. Moving south along the Indus river, the North becomes flatter and more hospitable, widening into the fertile plains of Punjab to the west and the Himalayan foothills of Uttar Pradesh and the Ganges river valley to the East. Cramped between these two states is the capital city, New Delhi.

The states of Gujarat, Maharashtra, Goa, and part of the massive, central state of Madhya Pradesh constitute West India. Extending from the Gujarat peninsula down to Goa, the west coast is lined with some of India's best beaches. The land along the coast is typically lush with rainforests. The Western Ghats separate the verdant coast from the Vindya Mountains and the dry Deccan plateau further inland. India reaches its peninsular tip with South India, which begins with the Deccan in the north and ends with

From top. Varanasi. Slumdog Millionaire, courtesy of Fox Searchlight. Taj Mahal, courtesy of Getty Images.

Cape Comorin. The states in South India are Karnataka, Andhra Pradesh, Tamil Nadu, and Kerala, a favourite leisure destination for both locals and international travellers.

Musical film is massively popular in India (and globally) with the Bollywood film industry, producing more films than Hollywood, and still largely based in Mumbai (formerly Bombay). The incumbent award-winning Bollywood formula of the song and dance routine, expertly choreographed fight scenes, emotion-charged melodrama, and larger-than-life heroes, churn out close to 600 commercial Hindi films annually, making India the most prolific film industry in the world. So it comes and no surprise that Mumbai is on the shortlist for travellers heading here. Other styles of American, British and Indian alliances filmed here have started to show India's cultural roots, not to mention stunning countryside in such comedies like Wes Anderson's 'Darjeeling Limited' and drama films like Danny Boyles' 'Slumdog Millionaire', have been recently filmed here, which have catapulted India to fame to younger audiences across the globe.

📖 **Fast Facts**

Capital: New Delhi.

Location: Bounded by the Indian Ocean, the Arabian Sea and the Bay of Bengal; bordered by Pakistan, China, Nepal, Bhutan Bangladesh and Myanmar in the vicinity of Sri Lanka, and the Maldives.

Population: 1.2 billion.

Religion: 80.5% Hindu; other religions are Muslim, Christians, Sikhs and Buddhists.

Languages: Official language Hindi, with English as secondary language.

⇛ Getting there and exploring around

Getting to India by air is usually the most convenient. India's major international airports are Mumbai (Bombay) and Delhi, though there are plenty of international flights also arriving in Calcutta and Chennai (Madras). The most popular overland routes between India and Nepal are Birganj-Raxaul, Sunauli-Gorakhpur and Kakarbhitta-Siliguri. The only border crossing currently open between India and Pakistan is between Lahore and Amritsar. This crossing can be done either by train or by road.

India's major domestic airline, the government-run Indian Airlines, has an extensive network. The country's international carrier, Air India, also operates domestically on the Mumbai (Bombay)-Delhi, Mumbai-Calcutta, Delhi-Calcutta and Mumbai-Chennai (Madras) routes.

The Indian Railways system is deservedly legendary and Indian rail travel is unlike any other sort of travel on earth. Indian Railways offers several services with tourists in mind, including the Darjeeling Himalayan Railway, which is nicknamed the 'Toy Train' and runs from New Jalpaiguri to Darjeeling; the purple-and-gold Golden Chariot, which connects Karnataka and Goa; and the most luxurious of them all, the Palace on Wheels, which departs from New Delhi and spend eight days touring Rajasthan from Jaipur to Agra. An eight-day journey on the luxurious Palace on Wheels starts at around $2,500. Normal rail travel can be uncomfortable and frustrating, but it is also an integral part of the Indian travel experience.

Buses vary widely from state to state, but there is often a choice of buses on the main routes - ordinary, express, deluxe, and even deluxe sleeper. Private buses tend to be faster, more expensive and more comfortable. Bus travel is generally crowded, cramped, slow and uncomfortable. This is the good news. The bad news is the rugby scrum you often need to negotiate in order to board, and the howling Hindi pop music which blares from the tinny speakers.

Local transport includes taxis, auto-rickshaws, cycle-rickshaws and tongas (horse-drawn carriages). Taxis may have meters, but don't expect them to be working in more than a handful of cities.

☼ Best time of year to visit

India experiences a range of climatic variations across its vast expanse. The monsoon season runs from July to September when rains sweep across the country with daily torrential downpours and a high possibility of flooding making travel difficult. The hot season from March to June witness's temperatures that can soar above average making it unbearable and hazy.

The cooler months from October to March are the best times to visit as the weather is very pleasant with minimal rainfall in most places. It is in these six months that the country is in a celebratory mood and India travel becomes more festive. Most of India's well-known festivals take place around this time. There is Dussehra with fireworks and drama in the north while in the east, the Durga Puja is celebrated to depict the conquest of good over evil. Three weeks after Dussehra is Diwali, the festival of light, and there are a lot of lamps and firecrackers. In March is the colourful festival of Holi when there are friendly fights with coloured water and coloured powder. In addition to these major festivals, there are a number of local festivals like the

Rathyatra or the Chariot festival in Orissa, the harvest festivals in most parts of India, dance festivals at heritage sites, and a host of others held towards the end of the year. The largest camel fair is held in Rajasthan's Pushkar in November while Goa has its own version of the Mardi Gras in February.

? Must know before you go

Train etiquette. Pick up the key points of Indian train etiquette as quickly as possible, otherwise you'll find yourself hopelessly attempting to defend your own private space. There are a number of different classes and the Indian reservation system is a labyrinthine, but be patient. When booking tickets, take advantage of the tourist quota allotment you'll find it easier to reserve a seat this way.

Friends beware. Watch out for anyone being too friendly. Many people will befriend you to sell you something. For example around temples be aware of locals talking to you then expecting 500 rupees tips! Don't tell people this is your first time in India, this makes you a magnet!

A word on water. Bottled water should have a hard plastic seal that you have to break when you unscrew the top. Stay away from bottles with only cellophane seals. Either Bailey's or Yes has both the hard plastic seal and expect to pay about 12-15 rupees a bottle, and finally DON'T DRINK THE WATER IF IT SMELLS BAD.

📷 Highlights

Desert Safari. Rajasthan whose major portion is covered by desert, is renowned for its desert safaris, explore the Thar Desert by camel or jeep.

Delights of Deli. Visit the largest residence of any Head of the State in the world, the Rashtrapati Bhavan (also once known as Viceroy's House).

Watching wildlife. Go 'Tiger Spotting' in Bandipur National Park, Karnataka, one of the regions best known sanctuaries.

Markets in Mumbai. Visit Mangaldas market, traditionally home to traders from Gujarat, is a great place to browse for Indian textiles and traditional clothes, such as duppatas (the long scarves).

★ Star Spotting

Film city of Maharashtra is located in the outskirts of the city at Goregaon where entry is strictly restricted for the civilians but you can achieve a pass if you have good connections with any of the film crew. You can see a live shooting going on there and also recognize few faces of the celebrities.

Genre: Romantic Comedy
Destination: Rajasthan

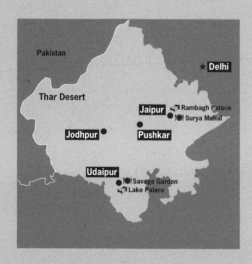

✦ Regional Information

The magic of vibrant Rajasthan - its rich heritage, colourful culture, exciting desert safaris, shining sand-dunes, amazing variety lush forests and varied wildlife - makes it a destination nonpareil. Rajasthan is often portrayed as one vast open-air museum, with its relics so well preserved that it delights even the most skeptical traveller. No wonder it's been popular for filmmakers both locally and internationally.

It's an incredible destination for the outdoor-tourist too – take a safari on horses, camels, elephants or even in jeeps, with the Aravalis - India's oldest mountain range as the backdrop. Feast your eyes on spectacular sand-dunes, take the tiger trail, or just watch the birds in the wetlands. You can also choose to pamper yourself in the lavish heritage properties.

It is situated in the north western part of India and shares geographical boundaries with Punjab, Haryana, Uttar Pradesh, Madhya Pradesh and Gujarat in India, and has a long international boundary with Pakistan. Being the driest part of India, it is home the Thar Desert, and fascinating cities, Udaipur, Jodhpur and Jaipur.

Udaipur is the pearl of India, the entrancing 'City of Dawn'. Here are lakes that come as a surprise in sandy Rajasthan and forested hills where wildlife still abounds. Udaipur derives it name from its founder Maharana Udai Singh of Mewar, who chose this place as a replacement for his earlier capital. Built around the azure waters of the lake Pichola, Udaipur, with its ornately decorated palaces and exquisitely laid out lakeside gardens, has captivated and enthralled people all over the world. It has also made its presence felt in the movie world when James Bond's Octopussy was shot in its plush and breathtaking locales. The piece de resistance of Udaipur is undoubtedly the Lake Palace hotel situated in the middle of crystal clear waters of the famous Pichola Lake. Key places to also visit are City Palace/Museum, Jagdish Temple, Saheliyon Ki Bari, and further away is the great fort of Chittorgarh, the spectacular temples of Mount Abu and the splendid palaces of Dungarpur.

Jodhpur is the second largest city in Rajasthan. It was formerly the seat of a princely state of the same name, it was the capital of the kingdom known as Marwar, featuring many palaces, forts and temples, set in the stark landscape of the Thar desert.

It is known as the Sun City for the bright, sunny weather it enjoys all year. It is also referred to as the Blue City due to the indigo tinge of the whitewashed houses around the Mehrangarh Fort. Jodhpur lies near the geographic centre of Rajasthan state, which makes it a convenient base for travel. The lifestyle in Jodhpur is unusually fascinating with folks wearing lovely multihued costumes and artistically designed dresses. Folk Women wear wide gathered skirts and hip-length jacket, with three-quarter length sleeves, covering the front and back. The colourful turbans worn by the men add more colour to the city. Surprisingly it was from here that the popularly worn baggy-tight, horse riding trousers – 'Jodhpurs' took their name.

The Thar Desert of Rajasthan is situated partly in India and partly in Pakistan. Also known as the 'Great Indian Desert', Thar covers an area of approximately 200,000 square km, and constitutes one of the five major physical divisions of India, the other being Himalayas, Northern Plains, Central Plateau and the Eastern and Western Coastal Plains. It occupies the western and north-western parts of the state of Rajasthan. Most of the sand dunes are forever in motion and keep on changing their shapes and sizes. The desert tract receives low and erratic rainfall annually, ranging from about 4 inches (100 mm) or less in the west to about 20 inches (500 mm) in the east. The maximum rainfall is received during the period of July to September. A tour of the Rajasthan Thar Desert is a must for any traveller. Various companies offer both camel and jeep safari's.

Jaipur, popularly known as 'Pinkcity', was designed in accordance with Shilp Shastra - an ancient Hindu treatise on architecture - Jaipur follows a grid system. The wide straight bazaars, raastaas (streets), galis (lanes), mohallas and uniform rows of shops on either side of main bazaars are arranged in nine rectangular city sectors called chaukris. Encircled by a formidable wall, Jaipur was the only planned city of its time, and forms part of the famous Golden Triangle Tourist circuit that also includes Delhi and Agra. Most travellers tour this city due to the architectural wonders, majestic forts and beautiful havelis (mansions).

Another popular tourist attraction in Jaipur is the Hawa Mahal. Built by Maharaja Sawai Pratap Singh in 1799, the purpose of this intricately carved five-storey Mahal was to allow women from royal families to observe the processions passing on the road below. Hawa Mahal also provides magnificent views of Jantar Mantar, City Palace and the famous local market below.

Genre: Romantic Comedy
Destination: Rajasthan

The Darjeeling Limited (2007)

The Darjeeling Limited directed by Wes Anderson, and starring Owen Wilson, Adrien Brody, and Jason Schwartzman, tells the story of three estranged brothers who reunite in Jodhpur to embark on a spiritual journey across India aboard the titular train. Plans get derailed, however, when a chain of events leaves them stranded in the middle of the desert with nothing but baggage—emotional or otherwise. Although the film didn't receive box office billions, in typical Anderson style the film is visually stunning — so it's only natural that his cross-country Indian adventure inspires travel. The majority of the film was shot in the Rajasthani desert in northwest India, a place which Anderson himself hadn't even visited until after he wrote the script.

You won't find the Darjeeling Limited train or the Bengal Lancer in India; they don't exist, although there is a train named 'Darjeeling Mail' that operates between Kolkata and Siliguri, the nearest broad gauge station to Darjeeling. The trains featured in the film are actually part of Indian Railways' North Western Railway, dressed up to fit the director's madcap vision. Anderson and a small crew actually shot for three months on a train with its own engine on live tracks. They gutted 10 coaches, redecorated the interiors with Indian crafts and shot most of the scenes on a moving train creeping across the Thar Desert in Rajasthan. If you've ever travelled on an Indian train, you realise how extraordinary this is - just buying a ticket used to be a full day's work. Negotiating the use of your own train on live tracks would have been a nightmare but the film benefits enormously.

The film's journey leads its stars to a monastery in the Himalayas, scenes which were filmed in Udaipur, India's 'city of lakes.' The city is full of elaborate palaces, many of which have been converted to luxury hotels, including the opulent

Taj Lake Hotel, which was also featured in the James Bond flick, 'Octopussy' - the rest of the film was shot in Jodhpur.

Stylish Place to Stay

Lake Palace, Udaipur
Since Udaipur is a city of palaces, it's only natural that you'd want to stay in one. If money isn't a concern, the best choice for a romantic stay would have to be the Taj Lake Palace. Often referred to as one of the world's most romantic hotels, it's a magical 250 year old white marble and mosaic summer palace, located in the middle of Lake Pichola. This place is in one word, incredible.

Delicious Place to Eat

Savage Garden, Udaipur
The trendy Savage Garden has plenty of character, with midnight-blue walls and a soothing courtyard setting, located in an old 18th century house which was lovingly restored using traditional techniques and local craftsmanship. There's an admirable mélange of Indian and continental dishes, including some inventive fusion fare.

Genre: Romantic Comedy
Destination: Rajasthan

Holy Smoke (1999)

Holy Smoke! is an Australian drama film directed by Jane Campion, who co-wrote the screenplay with her sister Anna. The movie sets up this drama with a brief series of scenes in which Ruth (Kate Winslet), a young Australian woman, travels in India, meets a guru, and becomes enlightened (literally, she seems to glow with a yellowish light when the guru touches her forehead during an introductory gathering). Her family hears of this turn of events through Ruth's astonished best friend, and they quickly act on the belief that she's been brainwashed, hiring (for $10,000) an expert 'exit counsellor' from the U.S named P.J. Waters (Harvey Keitel). Always dressed in black, seemingly self- assured, and occasionally imperious, he instructs them to lure Ruth to an isolated hut in the Australian outback, where he proceeds to hold her captive for three days, the usual duration of such 'treatment.' This fabulous, quirky film shows off some of India's great scenery, filmed in Pushkar, Jaipur and New Delhi.

Stylish Place to Stay

Hotel Rambagh Palace, Jaipur
Rambagh Palace was once the hunting lodge of the Maharaja of Jaipur and later his residence; it was converted to a palace hotel. The splendid architecture surrounded by 47acres of landscaped garden, sports an outstanding blend of Rajput and Mughal style. After a meticulous renovation and refurbishment, Rambagh Palace retains its old grandeur. A stay in Rambagh Palace would give you a fair idea of the degree of grandeur and opulence the royal family of Jaipur used to live. Rambagh Palace has played host to some of the world's renowned celebrities such as Mick Jagger.

Delicious Place to Eat

Surya Mahal, Jaipur
Although only used for evening meals during the winter season, the courtyard adjoining this all-day fine dining restaurant at Rajvilas is arguably the most romantic place to have dinner in Jaipur. Lit by huge burning braziers, the courtyard features a raised platform where beautiful Rajasthani women give a short performance of their traditional dance. You can sample the tastes of the region with a Rajasthani thali (multicourse platter), or, if you're up for something spicy, its quite a formal place so wear something smart.

Genre: Epics + Historical
Destination: Delhi

✛ Regional Information

It's hard to think of Delhi as anything but the capital of India but for a surprisingly long time Delhi was not the hot seat of power. Having said that, however, it's also true that Delhi was never exactly a sidekick on the scene of Indian history. Delhi is a vibrant melting pot; you'll hear a variety of lingo, the most common being Hindi, English, Punjabi and Urdu. In terms of its layout, Delhi encapsulates two very different worlds, the 'old' and the 'new', each presenting deliciously different experiences. Spacious New Delhi was built as the imperial capital of India by the British; rambunctious Old Delhi served as the capital of Islamic India. Travellers can easily dip into both, spending half the day immersing themselves in history at the dramatic Red Fort, Jama Masjid and medieval bazaars of Old Delhi, and the other half reviving themselves over a coffee at one of New Delhi's swanky cafés and bars.

One of the city's major festivals is perhaps one of the attractions of this city. Diwali, the religious Festival of Lights, is a time of mass celebration and there are plenty of other options, including the unique Kite Flying Festival, which marks a period where Delhi citizens celebrate with the flying of kites, a powerful symbol of freedom. A particularly fun festival to attend is the two-day International Mango Festival, a Delhi speciality that sees people travelling from all over to celebrate all things mango - not to be missed by big fans of the exotic fruit.

Today tourism in Delhi revolves mostly around these majestic monuments and heritage sites. During the Mughal rule, a number of majestic monuments were constructed by Mughal kings to display the pomp and splendor of the Mughal Empire. There were also other Indian rulers who patronized artisans. Today these monuments have become places of attractions in Delhi.

Genre: Epics + Historical
Destination: Delhi

Delhi is home to one of the worlds well known palaces 'The Viceroy palace' (also known as Rashtrapati Bhawan) and is befittingly the crowning glory of the British Empire and architecture in India. Today, it is perhaps India's best known monument after the Taj Mahal and the Qutub Minar. Bigger than the Palace of Versailles, it cost a whopping £12,53,000 and now houses the President of India. It is unquestionably a masterpiece of symmetry, discipline, silhouette, colour and harmony.

The most outstanding feature of the palace – you can spot it while you are mile away – is the huge neo-Buddhist copper dome that rises over a vast colonnaded frontage. Beneath the dome is the circular Durbar Hall 22.8m in diameter. The coloured marbles used in the hall come from all parts of India. The Viceroy's throne, ceremonially placed in this chamber, faced the main entrance and commanded a view along the great axial vista of Kingsway (now Rajpath). At present the hall is the venue of all official ceremonies such as the swearing in of the Prime Minister, the Cabinet and the Members of Parliament. It is in this very chamber that the President annually confers the Arjuna Awards for Excellence. After India became independent, the sheer size of the building overwhelmed its new keepers. Mahatma Gandhi suggested it be turned into a hospital. Thankfully, nobody took him seriously. The Durbar Hall served as a museum for several years till the building which now houses the National Museum was completed.

Rajpath meaning 'King's Way' is the ceremonial boulevard running from Rashtrapati Bhavan through Vijay Chowk and India Gate to the National Stadium. The New Delhi avenue is lined on both sides by lawns with rows of trees and ponds. Unarguably, the most important stretch of road in India, where the annual Republic Day parade takes on January 26, Rajpath goes straight towards Raisina Hill, India's administrative centre. Celebration of India becoming a republic and showcase of India's cultural diversity are celebrated here, and it is also used for funeral processions of important India's political leaders, (incidentally the opening scene of the movie Gandhi starts at Rajpath).

Gandhi Smritri (formerly Birla House or Birla Bhavan), is a museum dedicated to Gandhi where he spent the last 144 days of his life before he was assassinated on January 30, 1948. It was originally the house of the Indian business tycoons, the Birlas. It now houses the Eternal Gandhi Multimedia Museum, where the basic aim and objective is to propagate the life, mission and thoughts of Mahatma Gandhi through various socio-educational and cultural programmes. The museum in the building houses a number of articles associated with Gandhi's life and death. Visitors can tour the building and grounds, viewing the preserved room where Gandhi lived and the place on the grounds where he was shot while holding his nightly public walk.

Genre: Epics + Historical
Destination: Delhi

Gandhi (1982)

A beautiful biopic film based on the life of Mahatma Gandhi, who led the nonviolent resistance movement against British colonial rule in India during the first half of the 20th century. In 1893, as a young lawyer, Gandhi is thrown off a South African train for being an Indian and travelling in a first class compartment. Gandhi realizes that the laws are biased against Indians and decides to start a non-violent protest campaign for the rights of all Indians in South Africa. After numerous arrests and the unwanted attention, the government finally relents by recognizing rights for Indians, though not for the native blacks of South Africa. After this victory, Gandhi is invited back to India, where he is considered something of a national hero, and together with his new status is urged to take up the fight for India's independence from the British Empire.

The film was directed by Richard Attenborough and stars incredible British actor Ben Kingsley as Gandhi; the film was also given the Academy Award for Best Picture and won eight Academy Awards in total. This stunning film really makes you fall in love with Gandhi and India, if anything inspires you to travel, it is this film.

The film which was made almost entirely in India shows off some of India's important monuments and countryside, and scenes were also shot in South Africa. The film opens with Gandhi's assassination, which was filmed on the spot where Gandhi was actually shot, in the gardens of Gandhi Smritri, New Delhi. The next scene, his funeral, is one of the greatest scenes in cinematic history. Attenborough managed to recreate Gandhi's funeral on January 31st, 1981, the 33rd anniversary of the actual funeral. It is estimated that nearly 400,000 people were on hand to be a part of the filming. This film was made before computer generated images, so the funeral scene is probably the last live action

crowd of that magnitude that will ever be filmed. More filming took place at the Aga Khan Palace, Pune Nagar Highway, southeast of Mumbai, where Gandhi was interred during the Quit India Movement in 1942. It's now a Gandhi Memorial, open to the public.

Stylish Place to Stay

Master B&B, New Delhi
This gorgeous guesthouse is an oasis in Delhi where the roof top terrace can be used for unwinding and enjoying a light meal. Run by a lovely friendly couple who have worked hard to create a home like atmosphere. This place also has Reiki healing and yoga for the weary traveller.

Delicious Place to Eat

Punjabi by Nature, Delhi
Punjabi by Nature, has 5 venues, our favourite is the Raja Garden, which has a beautiful ambience, offering the very best North Indian cuisine. Signature dishes include Gol Guppa Shots, inspired by the local popular street food, which are basically puffed balls filled with a tangy spicy tamarind sauce. Personal favourites also include Tandoori Gobhi, Kofta Dilkhush, Dal Makhni and the rich Pineapple Raita

Opposite page. Top. Langur Monkey, Bandipur National Park, courtesy of Dreamstime.

Genre: Action + Adventure
Destination: Karnataka

✦ Regional Information

The South Indian state of Karnataka is a lot less travelled than its neighbours Kerala and Tamil Nadu, but more and more tourists are starting to discover its beautiful beaches, temple towns, wildlife and fascinating historical sites.

Its large impressive city Bangalore, is a great place to stay while exploring the region. Known as the 'Garden City' for its numerous lush gardens and 'Silicon Valley' for its IT status, Bangalore is one of the most happening cities in the country. What lures people to the city is its ever-pleasant climate, tourist attractions and a glamorous nightlife.

The Bangalore Palace, a replica of the Windsor Castle of England, is also the work of an architectural genius. Adding to the religiousness of the city are the St. Mary's Basilica the oldest church in the city, and the ISKCON Temple dedicated to Krishna which strives to blend modern with spiritual. Both the city and its economy have been growing fast, even though it is still a crowded and chaotic, Bangalore is filled with Western stores, coffee shops, restaurants and cinemas. Popular shopping areas include Brigade Road, M.G. Road and Commercial Street. And if the chaos in Bangalore gets too much, another city worth visiting while in Karnataka is Ramanagaram, just 48 kms from Bangalore.

Ramanagaram, and Savandurga is a haven for rock climbers with its rocky terrain and hills, there are the climbs called Wanakkal wall ('Gabbar ki asli pasand', 'labour pain') on the Rainbow wall ('UIAA', 'Kalia'), on the Anna Thamma Rock ('Darkness at Dawn', 'Black Diamond'). It is also famous for its historical temples on the hilly region, stone and granite quarries, silk cocoon industry, industrial belt at Bidadi Industrial Area, and also a great shooting location for action filled movies. Ramanagaram is one of the famous shooting locations for Indian films. The famous 'Sholay' movie has been filmed here, and 'A Passage to India' by David Lean was filmed on the Ramadevara Betta. Very few organised treks are conducted here and usually, it is an unplanned trek by a group of avid explorers. Bangalore Mountaineering Club conducts organised treks

and adventure trips all around Karnataka and a few other places in South India. They also conduct rock-climbing and trekking tours in Ramanagaram and other surrounding hillocks. Get in touch with them if you are interested in exploring Ramangaram's hills.

Travellers who love the outdoors and wildlife may head towards the Bandipur National Park to spot tigers, elephants or deers. Situated on the Mysore-Ooty road, Bandipur is part of Project Tiger, which is one of India's best known sanctuaries, and is an important reserve. It is located in the Chamarajanagar district of southern Karnataka, and is contiguous with the Mudumalai National Park in the neighbouring state of Tamil Nadu, the Wynad Wildlife Sanctuary in Kerala, and the Nagarhole National Park to the northwest. It is home to around seventy tigers and over three thousand Asian elephants, along with leopards, dholes, gaur and sloth bears. There are plenty of accommodation options inside the park, making it possible to kick back on the veranda with a cold drink while watching Langur monkeys hop by against a view of the Nilgiri Mountains.

For travellers looking to veer off the beaten track for a beach trip, should head towards Gokarna. First discovered by backpackers, Gokarna has now become a destination for travellers looking for quieter beaches in India. Gokarna itself is a small town and an important pilgrimage centre, but most tourists head to its four beaches: Kudle, Om, Half Moon and Paradise. Originally the beaches offered little more than bamboo huts and simple beach shacks, but accommodation and dining options are growing and there is even a brand new resort on Om Beach.

This page from left. Iyengars Bakery, Bangalore. Sholay, courtesy of raremovieimages.com. **Opposite page from left.** Bangalore Palace, courtesy of Dreamstime. Bedroom in the Purple Lotus, courtesy of Purple Lotus.

Genre: Action + Adventure
Destination: Karnataka

Sholay (1975)

Sholay is an Indian film directed by Ramesh Sippy and is the biggest hit in the history of Bollywood, India's Hindi film industry. The movie, shot in the rocky terrain of Ramanagaram, is the story of two petty criminals hired to capture, for a bounty, a ruthless dacoit by the name of Gabbar Singh. When first released, the film was declared a commercial disaster.

Word of mouth convinced movie-goers to give the film a chance and soon it became a box-office phenomenon, grossing $160 million.

The film was a lavish production for its time. It took two and a half years to make; it went Rs. 300,000 over budget. Much of the film was set in the rocky terrain of Ramanagaram, though the filmmakers had to build a road from the Bangalore highway to Ramanagaram for convenient access to the sets. In fact, one part of Ramanagaram town was renamed 'Sippynagar' after the director of the movie. Even to this day, a visit to the 'Sholay rocks' (where the movie was shot) is offered to tourists travelling through Ramanagaram (on the road between Bangalore and Mysore).

Stylish Place to Stay

Hill View Resort, Ramanagaram
Don't let the word 'resort' put you off. This place is the only place which offers views of 'Sholay Rocks', and is a great location for exploring the nearby countryside.

Delicious Place to Eat

Iyengars Bakery, Bangalore
If you're just planning on spending a day visiting the Ramanagaram hills, then take a picnic from the fabulous bakery Iyengars, which specialises in local pastries, sticky sweets, cakes and muffins. Iyengars Bakery was started in 1981 in the Austin town locality of Bangalore, as a small retail outlet. Over the years, it has grown to become a major landmark in the area. It was the first of its kind to introduce live baking in the city, so that the customers were able to see their favourite products in the making.

Genre: Action + Adventure
Destination: Karnataka

▓ A Passage to India (1984)

A Passage to India, director David Lean's final film (for which he also received editing credit), breaks no new ground cinematically, but remains an exquisitely assembled film. Based on the novel by E. M. Forster, the film is set in colonial India in 1924. Adela Quested (Judy Davis), a sheltered, well-educated British woman, arrives in the town of Chandrapore, where she hopes to experience 'the real India'. Here she meets and befriends Dr. Aziz (Victor Banerjee), who, despite longstanding racial and social taboos, moves with relative ease and freedom amongst highborn British circles.

The Marabar Caves used in the film are based on the Barabar Caves, some 35 km north of Gaya, in the state of Bihar. Lean visited the caves during pre-production but found them un-photogenic; concerns about bandits were also prevalent. Instead he used two separate hills (Savandurga and Ramadevarabetta) in Ramanagaram, where much of the principal filming occurred, other scenes were filmed in the Bangalore Palace, and some interiors were shot at the Shepperton Studios in Surrey.

◥ Stylish Place to Stay

Purple Lotus, Bangalore
Located in the heart of Bangalore, this boutique hotel has just 20 spacious suites and incredible views from the rooftop garden. Its convenient locations (near to all the local bars and restaurants) and friendly hospitality makes it rival all the 5 star chain resorts in the city.

⦿ Delicious Place to Eat

Kanua, Bangalore
The restaurant Kanua is an attempt to revive the art of ancient Karnataka cuisine. Kanua derives its name from a rice breed which has lost its identity in this world of commercialisation. Kanua offers some authentic Karnataka dishes such as Chicken Ghee Roast, Kane Rawa Fry and Vine Spinach. Kanua is out there to give you the true essence of Karnataka cuisine as it used to be. Service is quick and pleasant, and easy on the wallet as well.

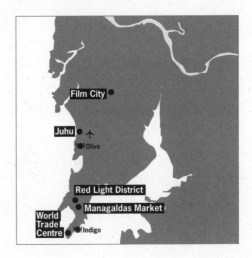

Focus On...
Mumbai

Maharashtra is the leading industrial state of India, and its capital Mumbai also happens to be the commercial capital of India, which also serves as the focal point of the Indian film industry, known as 'Bollywood'.

The Bollywood is world's largest film industry and was named after the capital city of the Hindi film Industry- Bombay (now Mumbai). Over the years this industry has become a trend settler and brought the latest fashion attires on streets, raises the issues on social cultural aspects and give judgements on what is right and what is wrong. It is also right to say that where there is films there is fashion. The Bollywood dictates the norms and people follow it silently. Every person has a role model in this film industry that he imitates and wishes to be like in his style of dressing, hair style and talking and physical appearance in general. This glamorous world attracts thousands of persons who are looking for a shortcut to stardom and livelihood. Definitely some people succeeded in making the mark in the film industry and are today famous artists but many vanished without a trace. Such is a tale of our silver screen, pay a visit to Mumbai and feel the heat of Bollywood charm.

Watch the shooting of the Bollywood movies the most happening in the Mumbai city. In the film city you can find the replica of every thing from fountains to lakes, buildings and forts that deceive the eyes of every one who took it as real. You will not surprised to even find even Switzerland in the green valleys of the Film City. Experience the live shooting of the upcoming blockbusters. And for anyone wanting to 'get involved' Bollywood nights are notoriously sociable, though the action in this 24-hour city doesn't get going until at least 10.30pm. In the centre of the city, the swanky Indigo restaurant and bar is usually packed cheek to famous cheek with screen stars, while uptown in Pali Hill, the Moroccan tent at Olive is the place to be seen.

Golden Globe film winner, Slumdog Millionaire (2008), directed by Danny Boyle, was shot mainly in the Mumbai megaslums, and in shantytowns of Juhu, but scenes were also used of the Taj Mahal in Agra, Uttar Pradesh. According to the film makers, shooting a film like Slumdog Millionaire was especially complicated, partly because of the scene locations that were chosen — like the Red Light District and the train station — which were known to be dangerous locations. Even though the filmmakers and film has received some criticism for the way it portrays India, the film has thought to have brought mega tourism to the slums of Mumbai.

Mumbai is also known for its exclusive boutiques, ethnic markets and mini bazaars which have made Mumbai a shopper's paradise. Most of the handicrafts Emporia and bazars are located in the downtown area. Crawford Market, Chor Bazar (Thieves Market), Mangaldas Market, World Trade Centre, Flora Fountain, Colaba Causeway, Oberoi Shopping Centre, Breach Candy, Linking Road and Zaveri Bazar are the main shopping centres in Mumbai.

(i) Stylish Essentials

General Information

General Tourist Information
www.incredibleindia.org
E. contactus@incredibleindia.org

Air India
www.airindia.com

Indian Airlines
www.indian-airlines.nic.in

General Train Enquiries
www.indianrail.gov.in

Darjeeling Himalayan Railway
T. +91 354 200 5734
E. director.dhr@gmail.com

Bus/overland Travel Information
www.indiatransit.com

The Palace on Wheels
www.thepalaceonwheels.com
T. +91 11 4686 8686
E. lawrence@nda.vsnl.net.in

Golden Chariot Train
www.goldenchariottrain.com
T. + 91 11 4686 8686

India by Road
Buses & Tours
www.indiatransit.com

Durga Puja Festival
www.durga-puja.org
E. festivalsindex@yahoo.com

Diwali Festival
www.diwalifestival.org
E. festivalsindex@yahoo.com

Rajasthan

General Tourist Information
www.rajasthantourism.gov.in

Jaipur Tourist Information
www.jaipur.org.uk

Thar Desert Safari
www.thardesertsafari.com
T.+91 151 252 1661

Palace Rambagh
www.tajhotels.com/Palace/Rambagh
T. +91 141 2211 919
E. rambagh.jaipur@tajhotels.com

Surya Mahal
www.suryamahal.com
T. +91 141 2369840
E. suryamahal@indiatimes.com

Lake Palace Hotel
www.tajhotels.com
T. +91 294 2428800
E. lakepalace.udaipur@tajhotels.com

Savage Garden
www.savagegardenindia.com
T. +91 294 242 5440

Rajasthan Tours
www.fascinatingrajasthan.com
T. + 91 11 4059 0538

Rajasthan Safaris
www.rajasthansafari.net
T. + 91 11 41557252

Delhi

Gandhi Smriti
Tees January Road,
New Delhi
www.gandhismriti.gov.in
T. +91 11 23392710

Master B&B
www.master-guesthouse.com
T. + 91 11 28741089
E. info@master-guesthouse.com

Punjabi by Nature
Raja Garden
www.punjabibynature.in
T. +91 11 47178000

Karnataka

General Tourist Information
www.bangaloreindia.org.uk

Bangalore Mountaineering Club
www.bmcindia.org
T. +91 80 25271045
E. corporate@bmcindia.org

Tiger spotting trips
www.ecoindia.com
E. info@ecoindia.com

Somak Tours of Bangalore
www.somak.co.uk
T. 020 8423 3000 (UK enquiries)

Hill View Resort, Ramangaram
www.hillviewresorts.in
T. +91 80 23353662
E. reservations@hillviewresorts.in

Purple Lotus
www.purplelotus.in
T. +91 80 4005 6300
E. info@purplelotus.in

Iyengars Bakery, Bangalore
45, ORC Road, Austin Town
Bangalore 560047
www.iyengarsbakery.com
E. admin@iyengarsbakery.com

Kanua
Sarjapur Road, Near Wipro
Headquarters,Bangalore
T. +91 80 65374471
Open: 12.00–15.00 and
19.00–23.00

Project Tiger
www.projecttiger.nic.in

Madumalai National Park Tours
www.indiajungletours.com/madumalai-national-park.html
T. +91 11 25892698

Indigo restaurant and bar
4 Mandlik Road,
T. +91 22 236 8999

Olive
14 Union Park,
T. +91 22 605 8228

Mumbai Bollywood Tours
www.bollywoodtourpackage.com
T. +91 11 22714 577
E. info@specialholidays.net

World Trade Centre Mumbai
www.wtcmumbai.org
T. +91 22 66387272

Mangaldas Market
Sheikh Memon Street,
Near Crawford Market,
Mumbai, 400002
Open: Mon-Sat 11.30–20.00

Ta Prohm, Cambodia.

CAMBODIA

Phnom Penh | Siem Reap | Kandal Province |
Mekong River

CAMBODIA

Thailand
Laos
Siem Reap
Mekong River
Phnom Penh
Kandal Province
Vietnam
Sihanoukville
Kampot
Gulf of Thailand
South China Sea

🏆 Why is this place so special?

Ancient temples, empty beaches, mighty rivers, remote forests and only a handful of tourists, compared to the rest of south-east Asia. But the word is out - Cambodia has emerged from the decades of war and isolation, poverty and political instability. Those magical Angkor temples are drawing gaping travellers by the bus loads and Cambodia is well and truly back on the south-east Asian travel map.

Indeed, the country and Phnom Penh in particular is undergoing something of a renaissance. Often overshadowed by the traumatic events of its recent past, Cambodia as home of the Khmer culture remains one of the most important and exotic countries in South East Asia. The culture of Cambodia has had a rich and varied history dating back many centuries, and has been heavily influenced by India and China. Throughout nearly two millennium, Cambodians developed a unique Khmer religion influenced by Buddhism and Hinduism. Indian culture and civilization, including its language and arts reached mainland Southeast Asia around the 1st century A.D, it is generally believed that seafaring merchants brought Indian customs and culture to ports along the Gulf of Thailand and the Pacific while trading with China. The Khmer culture can be witnessed across the country, from decorations in the temples to traditional Khmer dance.

The successor-state of the mighty Khmer Empire - which ruled much of what is now Vietnam, Laos and Thailand - Cambodia boasts a rich culture, French-era capital and impressive natural scenery. The peace is young but relatively stable, and the country is slowly attracting the tourism currently sweeping neighbouring Vietnam. However, the proliferation of land mines and banditry in remote areas means the picture isn't all rosy, and for now the beaten path remains by far the one best travelled. The incredible culture and impressive historical sites are a recipe for tourism, so many luxury hotels have started emerging, especially in the Siem Reap area, so for travellers

From top. Praying Monk, Angkor. Angkor Wat. Lotus pond, Angkor Wat Village Resort.

looking for a real south east Asian experience, yet with a little luxury thrown in, then there is no better place than Cambodia. And Cambodia isn't just about temples, beautiful beaches scatter the relatively unknown coastline around Sihanoukville and pretty pagodas surround the Kandal Province.

Beautiful locations, low production costs and few governmental restrictions, make Cambodia attractive to filmmakers, although few international box office hits have actually been filmed here, other than adventure film 'Lara Croft: Tomb Raider', 'City of Ghosts' and a handful of epic, independent historical films like the 'Rice People'. The world is more than ready to see more of Cambodia on film, but with already a very established tourism industry, the question is whether Cambodia wants the attention.

📖 **Fast Facts**

Capital: Phnom Penh.

Location: Situated in South East Asia with land borders Thailand, Laos and Vietnam.

Population: 13.1 million.

Religion: Thervada Buddhism (97%), Islam, Christianity, Animism.

Languages: Khmer.

✈ Getting there and exploring around

Thailand is the most convenient gateway to Cambodia when travelling from outside the region, by flying via Bangkok; or alternatively through Vietnam where you can easily pick up tickets and passes from Ho Chi Minh City.

Cambodia shares one border crossing with Laos, six crossings with Thailand and eight with Vietnam. Visas are now available at all the land crossings with Laos, Thailand and Vietnam, so these don't have to be applied for in advance.

There is a river border crossing between Cambodia and Vietnam on the banks of the Mekong as well. There are regular fast passenger boats plying the route between Phnom Penh and Chau Doc in Vietnam, via the Kaam Samnor–Vinh Xuong border crossing. There are also a couple of luxurious river boats; running all the way to the temples of Angkor in Cambodia, and also a river crossing on the Mekong border with Laos, although most travellers use the road these days.

It is possible to use buses to cross into Cambodia from Thailand or Vietnam. The most popular way is a cheap bus via Bavet on the Cambodian side and Moc Bai in Vietnam. It is complicated to bring in a car across the border, but relatively straightforward to bring in a motorcycle, as long as you have a carnet de passage (vehicle passport). This acts as a temporary import-duty waiver and should save a lot of hassles when dealing with Cambodian customs.

Cambodia's many waterways are a key element in the country's transportation system. Traditionally the most popular boat services with foreigners are those that run between Phnom Penh and Siem Reap. The express services do the trip in as little as five hours, but the boats between Phnom Penh and Siem Reap are horrendously overcrowded and foreigners are charged almost twice the price of Khmers for the 'privilege' of sitting on the roof. It is not the most interesting boat journey in Cambodia, as Tonlé Sap Lake is like a vast sea, offering little scenery. The small boat between Siem Reap and Battambang is more rewarding, as the river scenery is truly memorable, but it can take forever. Domestic flights offer a quick way to travel around the country. There is currently only one domestic airline fully operational in Cambodia, Siem Reap Airways. There are up to five flights a day between Phnom Penh and Siem Reap and it is usually possible to get on a flight at short notice. However, tickets book out fast in peak season.

There are a variety of ways to get around the temples. In the height of the summer it does pay to hire a guide with a car with air conditioning, as the heat can be oppressive. Helicopters Cambodia operates scenic flights around Angkor, but can be chartered for any journey. Cambodia is a great country for adventurous cyclists to explore.

☼ Best time of year to visit

The ideal months climatically are December and January, when humidity levels are relatively low, there is little rainfall and a cooling breeze whips across the land, but this is also peak season when the majority of visitors descend on the country.

From early February temperatures keep rising until the killer month, April, when temperatures soar and often exceed 40°C. Some time in May or June, the southwestern monsoon brings rain and high humidity, cooking up a sweat for all but the hardiest of visitors. The wet season, which lasts until October, isn't such a bad time to visit, as the rain tends to come in short, sharp downpours. Angkor is surrounded by lush foliage and the moats are full of water at this time of year. If you are planning to visit isolated areas, the wet season is tough travelling. Some visitors like to coordinate their trip with one of the annual festivals, such as Bon Om Tuk (the water festival held in November) or Khmer New Year (which is celebrated in mid-April) and lasts for 3 days.

? Must know before you go

Beware of begging. There are many child beggars around the temples of Angkor, and with their angelic faces it is often difficult to resist giving them some money. Some will try and sell you something, others just want cash. However, giving to children beggars may create a cycle of dependency that can continue into adulthood and the children may not benefit directly from the money, as they are often made to beg by a begging 'pimp'.

Learn the lingo. Locals wherever you travel always appreciate a little effort to speak their language, and no where is truer than in Cambodia. Say a few words of Khmer, and locals will be absolutely over the moon; this also might help you to negotiate better with hotel room rates, and bargaining for gifts to take back home.

Rising early. Customary Cambodian teachings states that if a person does not wake up before sunrise he is lazy; you'll see many Cambodians eating breakfast at the crack of dawn and making there way to work even before the sun rises, so roads even this early are usually very busy!

Highlights

Central market in Phnom Penh. One of Phnom Penh's better market complexes. Set around a run-down 1930's art-deco building, it sells cheap bags, t-shirts, random souvenirs and food. It's a great place to test out your bargaining skills.

Temple sightseeing in Siem Reap. Visit and marvel at the stunning temples around Siem Reap, the most famous being Angkor Wat, which is simply incredible at sun rise. Cycle around or better still, see it from air with a helicopter.

Visit the sacred Angkor Chey Pagoda. Located in the Kean Svay district the pagoda is constructed with five peaks as the temple's peaks and you need to pass a 100m wooden bridge to reach it.

Float by riverboat. Take a riverboat down the Mekong River, whether it's an afternoon or a 7 day excursion, it has to be experienced.

 Star Spotting

Cambodia isn't a country famous for its celebrity following, but there are several 'hot spots' which have known to have been visited by global stars. Angelina Jolie is believed to have a house near Siem Reap which she frequents with her family, and Phnom Penh Hotel is said to be popular with local celebrities.

Genre: Crime + Gangster
Destination: Phnom Penh

✦ Regional Information

Phnom Penh is the vibrant bustling capital of Cambodia. Situated at the confluence of three rivers, the mighty Mekong, the Bassac and the great Tonle Sap, what was once considered the 'Gem' of Indochina. Despite Cambodia recovering from a devastating history, Phnom Penh is not overwhelmed with sadness, and the capital city still maintains considerable charm with plenty to see, and is rivalling neighbouring cities such as Bangkok and Saigon. Although it does not boast as many tourist attractions it has an appealing quality with friendly locals, big markets, and a variety of places to eat from street sides to restaurants serving different cuisines. Phnom Penh, is also in the midst of rapid change. Over the past few years the number of hotels have grown considerably and in the last year there had been a huge increase in the number of visitors. See the real 'original' city now, as it won't be the same in a few years.

The main sights in town include Wat Phnom from where you have great views over the city, the Silver Pagoda in the Royal Palace complex, where you can see the emerald Buddha and a Buddha made of solid gold. Originally a wooden structure, the palace was initially constructed in 1892 during the reign of King Norodom, but rebuilt in its present grandeur by King Norodom Sihanouk in 1962. And he spared no effort to make this a true embodiment of the brilliance of Khmer art and a rich of an ancient culture. More than 5300, 1.125 kilo silver tiles make up the floor of the Silver Pagoda, giving it its name among foreigners. The silver floor alone weighs over six tones.

In terms of museums, the National Museum is regarded as one of the best museums in the country and is hailed as one of the landmark destinations in the city that tourists cannot afford to miss. The museum dates back to 1917 and was built by the French colonial powers when they were ruling over Cambodia. The museum has been built keeping in mind the typical Khmerian style of architecture and has most amazing artifacts and traditional collections collected from all over the world.

The Tuol Sleng Museum is also worth a look if you are intrigued by the torturous past, a sight that brings back a not too distant past: the terror of the Khmer Rouge. The building was a Khmer Rouge prison and torture chamber - very few of the prisoners survived and more than 30,000 died here.

Other sights include the Phnom Temple, the Orchid Garden, and the famous central market. From fresh fruit, up to date electronic products to expensive silks, the Central Market has absolutely everything to offer its visitors a complete shopping experience. Although there are numerous markets in Phnom Penh providing the shopaholic with a diverse shopping experience the Central Market is tagged as the largest and one that sells products of superior quality. With a distinctive cross shaped central dome, Cambodia's biggest market is also known by locals as the new market or Psar Thmay in Khmer. Before the construction of the Central Market, the country's largest city Phnom Penh was restricted to an area amid the Riverside and Norodom Boulevard.

Any traveller heading to Cambodia will most likely pass through Phnom Penh as it is also the gateway to the rest of Cambodia, the world heritage site, and the largest religious complex in the world, the temples of Angkor in the west, the beaches of the southern coast and the ethnic minorities of the North-eastern provinces.

166_Cambodia

Genre: Crime + Gangster
Destination: Phnom Penh

 ## City of Ghosts (2002)

City of Ghosts was also the first major US film using Cambodia as a principal location since the 1965 film Lord Jim; co-written, directed by and starring Matt Dillon, about a con artist who must go to Cambodia to collect his share in money collected from an insurance scam.

Jimmy (Dillon) plays a conman who's been working for a fake insurance company in New York City that is being investigated by the FBI after it cannot pay claims that have poured in after a hurricane. Discovering that his mentor and the mastermind of the scheme, Marvin (Caan), has skipped the country and gone to Thailand, Jimmy boards a plane with the intention of trying to collect his money.

Once in Bangkok, Jimmy meets Joseph Kaspar (Skarsgård), a partner in the scheme who's living with his Thai katoey companion Rocky (Kyoza). Joseph informs Jimmy that Marvin has moved on to Cambodia, where he's planning an even greater scam. So Jimmy sneaks across the border and makes his way to Phnom Penh.

Filming locations included Phnom Penh, Battambang, Kep, Oudong and Phnom Chisor, a pre-Angkor ruin south of Phnom Penh. The film's climax was shot at the ghostly, run down Bokor Hill Station, (3 hours from Phnom Penh), which was once a French colonial-era retreat with a hotel and casino complex.

Stylish Place to Stay

Amanjaya Pancam, Phnom Penh
A beautiful boutique hotel, well located in the heart of the city, very close to restaurants and bars along the river and a 5 minute walk from the Royal Palace and National Museum; just outside the hotel door there are many tuk tuks eager to take you anywhere you want to go. Most rooms have balconies with view of the Mekong River.

Delicious Place to Eat

Frizz restaurant, Phnom Penh
Traditional Cambodian food such as salads, crepes, and very good fish amok, with also a few international dishes such as steak and Guinness pie. It has recently relocated to street 240, which is a tree lined avenue full of boutiques and shops selling quality silks, arts, crafts and gifts. They also run Cambodian cooking classes for those looking to experience something different!

Genre: Action + Adventure
Destination: Siem Reap

✦ Regional Information

Siem Reap province is located in northwest Cambodia. It is the major tourist hub in Cambodia, as it is the closest city to the world famous temples of Angkor (the Angkor temple complex is north of the city). The provincial capital is also called Siem Reap and is located in the South of the province on the shores of the Tonle Sap Lake, the greatest sweet water reserve in whole Southeast Asia. The name of the city literally means 'Siamese defeated', referring to the victory of the Khmer Empire over the army of the Thai kingdom in the 17th century.

At the turn of the millennium Siem Reap was a Cambodian provincial town with few facilities, minor surfaced roads and little in the way of nightlife. Tourism industry catered largely to hardy backpackers willing to brave the tortuous road from the Thai border on the tailgate of a local pick-up truck. There were a couple of large hotels and a handful of budget guesthouses, and Tuk-tuks and taxis were non-existent. Things have certainly changed in recent times. The proximity of the Angkor ruins turned Siem Reap into a boomtown in less than half a decade. Huge, expensive hotels have sprung up everywhere and budget hotels have mushroomed. Property values have soared to European levels and tourism has become a vast, lucrative industry. The Siem Reap of today is barely recognizable from the Siem Reap of the year 2000.

Angkor is by at large one of the main reasons travellers flock to Cambodia, made famous in the last decade by the Lara Croft Tomb Raider film. There are about 60 temple ruins in the Siem Reap area alone so you need to choose according to your schedule and level of interest. On the 'must see' list are the legendary ruins of Angkor Wat, the giant faces of Bayon and the Giant tree at Ta Prohm. The famous South Gate of Angkor Thom can be seen on route to Bayon. The site features some 30 Hindi and 20 Buddhist temples and many have been left to crumble into disrepair but are still

fascinating and unforgettable places to visit. At the heart of the site is the Hindi Phnom Bakheng temple with its 108 surrounding towers and the much-photographed Angkor Wat itself stands to the side in the jungle. Because of the sheer scale of the site it's recommended to hire a guide in Siem Reap over a few days, most speak excellent English and will help you plan your days efficiently. Other than cycling or by car, one of the most exhilarating ways to experience the vastness of the temples is by helicopter, or by hot air balloon.

It's very easy to get 'templed out' here after a few days, so there are other attractions in the area if you are staying longer. Such as visiting the Tonlé Sap Lake, which is the largest fresh water lake in south-east Asia. During the monsoon season between June and October the Tonlé Sap River reverses its flow and runs in the opposite direction, filling the Tonlé Sap Lake. The Tonlé Sap River is the only river in the world that flows in both directions. For those who enjoy their food, culinary tours and Khmer cooking classes, can also be arranged and many local restaurants also offer buffets with Khmer traditional dancing, which can be pretty good fun.

Opposite page. Top. Ta Prohm, Angkor.
Bottom. Monks at Angkor Wat. **This page.**
Deluxe double bedroom at Angkor Wat
Village Resort.

Genre: Action + Adventure
Destination: Siem Reap

🎬 Tomb Raider (2000)

Tomb Raider is the first film to be shot in
Cambodia since Peter O'Toole played Lord Jim
in the shadow of Angkor Wat in 1964 (one
reason why West wanted to film there). Since then,
however, the country has had other things on its
plate: bombed by the US during the Vietnam war,
ravaged by Pol Pot and his Khmer Rouge cadres
in the 1970s, under occupation by Vietnamese
troops in the 1980s and engulfed in civil war in
the early 1990s, it has long been a no-go area for
hardened backpackers, never mind unwieldy US
film crews. Roland Joffe's 'The Killing Fields'
(1984), which described the background to the
murder of some two million Cambodians by Pol
Pot's regime, was filmed in neighbouring Thailand.

So the impact of 'Tomb Raider' was very
significant. Cambodia has experienced something
of a renaissance, and judging by the impact on
tourism of the modestly successful Leonardo
DiCaprio vehicle 'The Beach', which triggered
a mini-invasion of Thailand's Phi Phi Leh island,
Angkor could be swamped with tourists for many
years to come.

The film is also good news for the
temples. The conservation authority responsible
for preserving and protecting the complex is
charging Paramount $10,000 per day for seven
days. Much of the money will go back into caring
for the temples themselves.

⛴ Stylish Place to Stay

Angkor Wat Village Resort, Siem Reap
An amazing little retreat near to the temples of
Angkor, with lodge style accommodation (which
look like wooden huts on stilts) are set among lush
tropical gardens and ponds. The hotel's restaurant,
Aarama serves the best of Indochine as well as
international dishes, while the Apsara Theatre
combines dinner with dance and musical
performances. Additional facilities include a
Jacuzzi, library with internet and spa located in an
exquisite wooden pavilion, and a pool to relax your
feet after a hard days' sightseeing.

🍴 Delicious Place to Eat

Amansara, Siem Reap
A chic, hip place to hang out, (and stay!) head to
the beautiful roof terrace with casual seating on
large scattered cushions. The terrace looks up to
a canopy of mature trees and is the ideal spot to
relax in the late afternoon and evening. Drinks,
snacks, tea and coffee are available.

Genre: Epics + Historical
Destination: Kandal Province

✈ Regional Information

There are many provinces in Cambodia and Kandal is one of the smallest of them.
It isn't hugely well known compared to the rest of Cambodia, but it worth a visit if you
have a long stay planned. This province lie's 20 kilometres to the south of Phnom Penh,
with its capital being Ta Khmao. Famous for its ancient history, one of the prime
attractions for tourists is Udong which was the capital of Cambodia between 1618
and 1866. This small town served as the Khmer capital before King Norodom moved
the capital south to Phnom Penh. Today it's an important pilgrimage destination for
Cambodians paying homage to their former kings. You can join them on the climb to
the pagoda-studded hilltop, site of the revered Vihear Prah Ath Roes assembly hall,
which still bears the scars of local conflicts from the Khmer Rouge era.

The province consists of the typical plain wet area for Cambodia, covering
rice fields and other agricultural plantations. The average altitude of the province is
supposedly not more than 10m above see level. The province also features two of
the biggest rivers of the country (actually they symbolize the provincial borders) the
Tonle Bassac and the mighty Mekong. The rice fields in the area may have been the
inspiration behind filming the 'Rice People' in this location.

Eighteen kilometres away from Phnom Penh, is Kien Svay - the Cambodian
leisure resort. Every weekend many Phnom Penh residents get away from it all and
relax by the water. Here they rent 'Water Houses' covered platforms built on stilts sunk
into the river, and picnic on the water. They are accessible by boat and the platform
owners take you there and back. There are also relaxing boat cruises that take you
around the resort area.

As Kandal province isn't far from Phnom Penh it is easily and quickly to enter, even if it's just a day trip. There is quite a bunch of places of interest such as Angkor Chey Pagoda, which is located at Ban Tey Dek commune, Kien Svay District with a total distance of 29km from Phnom Penh or 32,6km from Ta Khmao. The pagoda is constructed with five peaks as the temple's peaks. Before reaching the pagoda, we need to pass over a 100-meter wooden bridge; under the bridge, there is a big pond for keeping water during the dry season.

Behind the pagoda you'll see an artificial site located on the black hill characterised as resident of Neak Mean Bon or King. It is said that the black hill is a former palace, because they found ancient objects and equipment like bowls and pots characterizing ancient features. Now, the black hill has been organized and maintained by guards, because it relates to the belief in sacred objects there. Nowadays, Angkor Chey pagoda has a lot of local visitors, especially those, who cling to abstract belief; they go there to have themselves sacredly watered. In addition, Angkor Chey pagoda is surrounded with beautiful scenery offering cool shadows from the trees and a pleasant environment.

There are numerous restaurants and bars in Kandal. You can enjoy an authentic dinning experience which comes at reasonable rates, compared to other touristy areas. The people of Kandal (also all over Cambodia) prefer a stronger sour taste in their dishes, than Thailand. The dishes become spicier with the addition of Prahok. If you are yearning for some Chinese cuisine in Kandal, you won't be disappointed. A large number of Chinese restaurants are scattered all across Kandal, and you can't leave without taking a few sips of the famous Palm wine and rice wine in exotic bars in Kandal. At least the golden muscle wine offers you an authentic Khmer experience.

Opposite page. Wat Udong, Kandal Province, courtesy of Dreamstime. **This page from top.** Water Houses, Kien Svay, courtesy of Dreamstime. Anchor Beer.

Genre: Epics + Historical
Destination: Kandal Province

🎬 Rice People (1994)

Rice People is a 1994 Cambodian drama film directed and co-written by Rithy Panh. Adapted from the 1966 novel Ranjau Sepanjang Jalan (No Harvest But a Thorn), by Malaysian author Shahnon Ahmad, which is set in the Malaysian state of Kedah, Rice People is the story of a rural family in post-Khmer Rouge Cambodia, struggling to bring in a single season's rice crop. It was filmed in the Cambodian village of Kamreang, in the Kien Svay and Boeung Thom areas of Kandal Province near Phnom Penh, on the banks of the Mekong River. The film premiered in the main competition at the 1994 Cannes Film Festival and was submitted to the 67th Academy Awards, the first time a Cambodian film had been submitted as a possible nominee for Best Foreign Language Film.

🛏 Stylish Place to Stay

The Boddhi Tree Aram, Phnom Penh
Set in the heart of Phnom Penh's colonial district and within a short walk of both the Royal Palace and the riverfront, Boddhi Tree Aram is the most luxurious of the three Boddhi Tree properties in Phnom Penh. Its restaurant serves delicious breakfast on a terrace, and features equally good Asian and continental cuisine, including omelettes, fresh juices, smoothies and fruit.

🍽 Delicious Place to Eat

Kandal House, Phnom Penh
The menu at this tiny restaurant on the riverfront includes some delicious homemade pastas, salads and soups, plus a smattering of Asian favourites. Chilled Anchor draught is available in pints.

Focus On...
Mekong River

The Mekong is one of Asia's major rivers, and the twelfth longest in the world. Sometimes called the 'Danube of the East', it nurtures a great deal of life in its waters – and in the wetlands, forests, towns and villages along its path.

The Mekong's long journey begins in the Tibetan highlands. It flows through China's Yunan province, and then across Burma, Thailand, Laos and Cambodia before entering the sea from southern Vietnam. It's a journey of nearly 5,000 kilometres, or some 3,000 miles.

For the past 800 years, explorers from Kublai Khan to Frenchman Francis Garnier have sought to conquer the river and the region that surrounds it, sending warrior hordes south toward Cambodia's Angkor Wat or dispatching parties in dugout canoes north from Saigon (now Ho Chi Minh City). These early expeditions survived tigers, leeches, and quicksand, but never completely penetrated the Mekong Basin or reached the river's source, in Tibet.

An expedition cruise between Ho Chi Minh City and Siem Reap allows you to see more of the region in less time than on self-powered journeys. Pandaw Cruises runs two custom-built colonial-era teakwood steamers up and down the river. You'll float past Cambodia's capital, Phnom Penh, and go ashore to hike the country's Wat Hanchai hill, home to ancient Champa shrines. Onboard, languorous hours are spent sipping gin-and-tonics on the deck as the jungle drifts by.

Although no films have been produced featuring the Mekong in its entirety, (some films have used a few shots for scenes), there are up and coming films from independent film makers such as Khmer Mekong Films, which recently produced Vanished (2009) and Staying Single When (2007) which were filmed in nearby Kep and Angkor Wat, which will no doubt revive the Cambodian film industry in time.

ⓘ Stylish Essentials

General Information

General Tourist Information
www.tourismcambodia.com

Thai Airways
www.thaiaiways.co.uk
www.thaiaiways.co.uk
T. 0870 6060911
(UK reservations)
E. reservations@thaiairways.co.uk

Bangkok Airways
www.bangkokair.com
T. +44 1293 596 626
(UK reservations)

Siem Reap Airways
www.siemreapairways.com
T. +855 720022

Bus companies

Mekong Express Limousine
#87 Eoz, St. Sisowath Quay, Phnom
Penh, Cambodia.
T. + 855 23 427 519

GST Express Bus
#13 Street 142, Phnom Penh 12209
Cambodia.
T. +855 12 838-910

Capitol Tours
#14 Street 182, Phnom Penh 12258
Cambodia.
T. +855 23 217627

Boat companies

Khemara Express Boat
High Way No 5A In Front of Soksan
Club
T. +855 23 430 777

Royal Express Boat
Sangkat Sras Chork Khan Daun
Penh, Road No 5.
T. +855 23 725 538

Angkor Express Boat
Sisowath Squay International Phnom
Penh Port.
T. +855 23 426 892

Hang Chau Boat
Sisowath Squay International Phnom
Penh Port.
T. +855 12 883 542

Helicopters Cambodia
www.sokhahelicopters.com
T. +855 23 885 773

Phnom Penh

National Museum
Corner of Sts. 178 and 13
Phnom Penh, Cambodia
T. +855 23 211 753

Silver Pagoda
Between Streets 240 & 184
Phnom Penh 12202, Cambodia
T. +855 23 21 6666
Open: Daily from 8.00–11.00 and
14.30–17.00

Central Market
Neayok Souk
Phnom Penh, Cambodia

Amanjaya Pancam
www.amanjaya-pancam-hotel.com
T. +855 23 219 579
E. reservation@amanjaya-pancam-
hotel.com

Frizz Restaurant
67, Street 240, Phnom Penh,
www.frizz-restaurant.com
T. +855 23 22 09 53

Siem Reap

Hot Air Balloon Rides
T. + 855 012 520 810

Helicopters Cambodia
T. +855 012 814 500

Sokha Helicopters
T. +855 012 1848891.

Culinary tours and Khmer cooking classes

The River Garden Guesthouse
T. +855 (0) 63 963 400

Le Tigre de Papier
T. +855 (0) 12 659 770

Khmer Dance Theatres

Dead Fish Tower
T. +855 (0) 12 630 377

Apsara Theatre
T. +855 (0) 63 963 561

Amazon Angkor Restaurant
T. +855 (0) 12 966 988

Butterflies Garden Restaurant
T. +855 (0) 63 761 211

Angkor Wat Village Resort
www.angkorvillage.com
T. +855 63 963 361
E. welcome@angkorvillage.com

Amansara
www.amanresorts.com
T. + 855 63 760 333
E. amansara@amanresorts.com

Kandal province

Angkor Chey Pagoda
Ban Tey Dek commune,
Kean Svay District

The Boddhi Tree Aram
www.boddhitree.com
T. +855 (0)11 854 430
E. bookings@boddhitree.com

Kandal House
239 Sisowath Quay,
Riverside, Phnom Penh
T. + 855 012 525 612
E. kndalhouse@mobitel.com.kh

Mekong River

River trip along Mekong
www.discovermekong.com

**Riverboat excursion
down Mekong**
www.pandaw.com

Vancouver Harbour.

CANADA

Alberta | Ontario | Quebec | Vancouver

CANADA ● ● ●

🏆 Why is this place so special?

The expanse of Canada's natural beauty, from mountains and glaciers to secluded lakes and forests, is almost unparalleled worldwide. But Canada's allure is not just the great outdoors; Canada has cosmopolitan cities that are clean, safe and friendly with some of the finest dining in the world. In fact, Canada repeatedly is suggested as one of the world's most livable countries. Whether your interests are river rafting or live theatre, Canada won't disappoint.

The land occupied by Canada was inhabited for millennia by various groups of Aboriginal people. Beginning in the late 15th century, British and French expeditions explored, and later settled along, the Atlantic coast. France ceded nearly all of its colonies in North America in 1763 after the Seven Years' War.

A federation comprising ten provinces and three territories, Canada is a parliamentary democracy and a constitutional monarchy, with Queen Elizabeth II as its head of state. It is a bilingual and multicultural country, with both English and French as official languages both at the federal level and in the province of New Brunswick. One of the world's highly developed countries, Canada has a diversified economy that is reliant upon its abundant natural resources and upon trade—particularly with the United States, with which Canada has had a long and complex relationship.

Today, television, movies, music, news, and literature, available to Canadians is both American and Canadian in origin. Though many Canadians believe a unique distinct Canadian culture exists, even in an era of deep economic and cultural ties between the two nations. The Canadian film market was dominated by America for decades, although since the 1980s the Canadian film industry has blossomed. Vancouver in particular, has become known as Hollywood North, being a stage for films like 'Night at the Museum' (2006) and regions like Alberta have become popular for epic, historical films that require stunning backdrops, such as 'Legends of the Fall' (1994).

Canadian producers have also been very successful in the field of science fiction since the mid-1990s, with such shows as The X-Files, Stargate SG-1, the new Battlestar Galactica, and Smallville, all filmed in Vancouver. As with Hollywood, many Canadians are employed in the film industry, and celebrity-spotting is frequent throughout many Canadian cities.

Canada has also churned out a number of very successful actors and comedians such as Dan Aykroyd, Mike Myers, Jim Carrey, Rick Moranis and John Candy.

Canada's film industry is in full expansion as a site for Hollywood productions. Montreal, due to its European appearance, has served in a great variety of mainstream movies, attracting the loyalty of industry people such as Bruce Willis; and there are plans to build the world's biggest film studio on the outskirts of the city. The choice of location is allegedly due to cost, rather than a requirement for a 'Canadian atmosphere'. The frequent question of a Canadian, seeing a film crew on his or her local streets, is 'Which bit of the States are we pretending to be today?'

Fast Facts

Capital: Ottawa.

Location: Occupying most of northern North America, extending from the Atlantic Ocean in the east to the Pacific Ocean in the west and northward into the Arctic Ocean. Its land border with the USA is the longest in the world.

Population: 33,487,208.

Religion: Roman Catholic 42.6%, Protestant 23.3%, other Christian 4.4%, Muslim 1.9%, other 11.8%, none 16%.

Languages: English (official) 58.8%, French (official) 21.6%, other 19.6%.

Getting there and exploring around

Vancouver (YVR), Toronto (YYZ), and Montréal (YUL) serve as the dominant hubs for international flights, and are served by most international carriers including British Airways, Air France, Qantas, Singapore Airlines, Lufthansa, SAS, and many U.S. airlines. Smaller airports such as Calgary and Winnipeg also have some international flights, particularly in summer.

Air Canada the country's national airline, is by far the largest carrier in Canada; in 1999, it subsumed Canadian Airlines, giving it and its subsidiary companies dominance over internal and external Canadian air travel. You can fly direct to Canada with Air Canada from most major European airports, such as London.

Because Canada has the longest open border on earth, it makes sense that many U.S. based travellers will consider taking their own car to Canada as a road-trip destination. There are scores of border crossings between Canada and the U.S. However, not all border crossings keep the same hours, and many are closed at night. Before you set off to cross the border at a remote location, ascertain if it will be open when you arrive there. Canada has scores of rental-car companies, nevertheless, rental vehicles tend to get tight during the tourist season, from around mid-May through August. It's a good idea to reserve a car as soon as you can.

Getting to Canada by train is also possible. Amtrak can get you into Canada at a few border points, where you can connect up with Canada's VIA Rail system. Amtrak and VIA Rail both offer a North American Rail pass, which gives you 30 days of unlimited economy-class travel in the U.S. and Canada. Remember that the Rail pass doesn't include meals; you can buy meals on the train or carry your own food.

Getting around Canada by plane if you don't have a lot of time is the best option. Canada is undergoing a renaissance in regional air travel; Westjet offers the largest service area, with flights spanning the country from Victoria to St. John's.

Best time of year to visit

When to go to Canada depends a lot on what you plan to do when you get there. As average winter and summer high temperatures across Canada vary according to the location. Winters can be harsh in many regions of the country, particularly in the interior and Prairie provinces, which experience a continental climate, where daily average temperatures are near −15°C but can drop below −40°C with severe wind chills, great if you like the cold and want to ski!

As a general rule, spring runs mid-March to mid-May, summer mid-May to mid-September, autumn mid-September to mid-November, and winter mid-November to mid-March. Pick the season best suited to your tastes and temperament. Evenings tend to be cool everywhere, particularly near water. In late spring and early summer, you'll need a supply of insect repellent if you're planning on camping.

If you are planning on visiting a few festivals while you're there then you won't be disappointed as Canada is full of festivities most of the year. Though the best ones are; Winter Carnival in Quebec (February), Yukon Quest (one of the worlds top dog sledding events) also in February, Canadian Tulip festival in May, Stratford Festival throughout May – October, Calgary Stampede, a rodeo in July, and Toronto Film Festival in September.

? Must know before you go

Driving in Canada. In addition to having the proper ID to cross into Canada, drivers may also be asked to provide proof of car insurance and show car registration. Until the 1920s Canadians used to drive on the left, but now everywhere they drive on the right.

Crossing Borders. It's always a good idea to clean your car or your bags of perishable foodstuff before crossing the border; fruit, vegetables, and meat products may be confiscated and may lead to a full search of the car. Although firearms are allowed across the border only in special circumstances; handguns are almost completely outlawed!

Courteous Canadians. Don't be surprised by how friendly and polite Canadians are. It's a cliché built on truth, and will go out of their way to help you.

Highlights

Explore the outdoors. Head to Alberta's Rocky Mountains area, and enjoy the fresh, clean air while getting an adrenaline buzz hiking, skiing or climbing.

Experience Niagara Falls. One of the Seven Wonders of the World can be experienced by taking the classic Maid of the Mist boat to the base of the falls.

Old Montreal Tour. Enjoy a private 3-hour walking tour focusing on more than 360 years of history.

Dine in style in Vancouver. Vancouver has some of the world's finest restaurants, and freshest seafood.

★ Star Spotting

Spotting a celebrity in Vancouver has gotten a lot more common. Jessica Alba, Halle Berry, Hugh Jackman and more have explored the city when they're not filming, frequenting joints like Blue Water Café + Raw Bar (Alicia Silverstone, Jamie Lee Curtis, Uma Thurman), CinCin Ristorante (Ben Affleck, Naomi Watts, Macy Gray, Robin Williams, Justin Timberlake) and Tojo's Restaurant (William Shatner, Eddie Murphy, Morgan Freeman).

Genre: Epics + Historical
Destination: Alberta

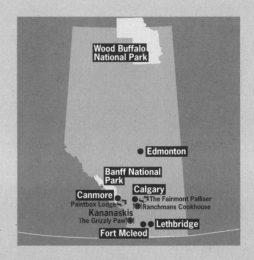

Wood Buffalo National Park
Edmonton
Banff National Park
Canmore
Paintbox Lodge
Kananaskis
The Grizzly Paw
Fort Mcleod
Calgary
The Fairmont Palliser
Ranchmans Cookhouse
Lethbridge

✦ Regional Information

The Alberta Rocky Mountain area is one of the most beautiful places on earth. Starting with the dynamic city of Calgary, to the stunning Banff National Park, Lake Louise, Kananaskis Country and Canmore in the south; there is a wealth of travel experiences to be enjoyed in Canada's largest mountain range. The attractions in this region are geared towards the outdoors, taking full advantage of the natural geography of the area. Downhill and alpine skiing, snowmobiling, rock climbing, hiking and wilderness camping are just a few of the many experiences. The small, mountain towns that are speckled throughout also add to the atmosphere, with their small gift shops, local restaurants and friendly inns.

Many films have been set in the Rockies, but it's the Western genre that puts the landscape to its best use, such films like Legends of the Fall, Brokeback Mountain, to The Assassination of Jesse James have all been filmed here. Southern Alberta's own style of frontier history, set amid unspoiled natural beauty, has made it a favourite backdrop for movies, from exacting period pieces to sweeping 'big country' dramas.

Calgary is an attractive city situated on the banks of the Bow River and close to Alberta's majestic Rocky Mountains, which make it a perfect stop-over point if you are heading that way. The Calgary Stampede is undoubtedly Calgary's best-known visitor attraction. This event, featuring a large parade and world-class rodeo, draws more than a million people each year. The host city of the 1988 Winter Olympic Games also takes pride in its sporting legacy and the Canada Olympic Park is a multi-purpose athletic facility designed for skiing, snowboarding, bobsleigh and luge during the winter and mountain biking during the summer.

West of Calgary about 20 km, south at Highway 22, is known as the Cowboy Trail, nestled between the Rocky Mountains and the Canadian prairie. For those who have longed to be a 'cowboy' after watching numerous 'Westerns' can saddle up and

stay on a ranch, experience a horseback trail or take part in an actual rodeo. There are many inns and saloons on route.

The town of Canmore, located in the Kananaskis country, west of Calgary, is a year-round destination, with a thriving arts community, golf, hiking, mountain-biking in summer and cross country skiing in the winter. For something a little daring, check out Wild Cave Tour's Canmore Caverns tour, where you'll descend into a cave on Grotto Mountain. Experienced guides will interpret the fascinating natural history. The pilot for Everwood starring Stacey Keach was filmed here, with Canmore's main street serving as Everwood's main drag.

Moose Mountain, flanking the town of Canmore, is the one climbed by the movie's two key characters in Brokeback Mountain, and their herd of sheep—it's very scalable. The average hiker can do the round trip to the peak in about six hours.

Banff National Park is a stone's throw west on the Trans-Canada Highway, centered around the world-famous mountain community of Banff, a vacation destination in its own category. Hollywood discovered this area more than 60 years ago, filming the backdrop to Spring Time in the Rockies in 1942, followed by The Emperor Waltz with Bing Crosby and River of No Return with Marilyn Monroe. Wandering the passageways of the famous Fairmont Banff Springs hotel, gleaning treasures from downtown boutiques, visiting art galleries, or exploring the spectacular landscape, or ride to the top of Sulphur Mountain on the Banff Gondola, are highlighted as some of the best things to do. A trip to Banff wouldn't be complete without a bit of luxury, so soak your muscles in the Upper Hot Springs a naturally heated pool amidst spectacular alpine scenery. Find the hot springs on Mountain Avenue, a few minutes south of the town.

Genre: Epics + Historical
Destination: Alberta

🎬 Legends of the Fall (1994)

The spectacular scenery of Alberta has made it a mecca for 'western' film shoots, including Legends of the Fall, the 1994 Oscar-winning film starring Brad Pitt and Anthony Hopkins. For the role of Tristan an epic tale of three brothers raised by their father in the wilderness in the early 1900's, Pitt is said to have had to learn how to ride. He must have taken to it. He was back to Alberta in 2005 for the filming of the Assassination of Jesse James. The Legends WWI scenes were filmed just north of Calgary and included serviceman from the Canadian forces to work with the locally-recruited extras. Right from the start of this film, Director Edward Zwick and Cinematographer John Toll, take us on a magnificent journey through some of the most breathtaking vistas, shot mostly on the Stoney Indian Reserve near Calgary. Not surprisingly, John Toll won an Academy Award for his breathtaking outdoor cinematography.

🛏 Stylish Place to Stay

The Fairmont Palliser, Calgary
A hotel with a lot of history. Opened in 1914 as one of the Canadian Pacific Railroad hotels, the Palliser is Calgary's landmark historic hotel, and remains its most visible expression of old-world luxury. Stay a night here and check out the ballroom where 250 Calgary residents were used as extras for a banquet scene in the film Assassination of Jesse James. Allegedly Brad Pitt, Angelina Jolie, Elton John have known to have stayed in the Royal Suite.

🍽 Delicious Place to Eat

The Grizzly Paw, Kananaskis
The Grizzly Paw is well known for having the best pub fare in the Rockies. They have fabulous sharing food which goes down perfectly with a pint. Don't forget the scrumptious deserts.

Opposite page, from left. Fairmont Palliser, courtesy of Dreamstime. Legends of the Fall, courtesy of Getty Images. **This page.** Brokeback Mountain, courtesy of ZML.

Genre: Epics + Historical
Destination: Alberta

Brokeback Mountain (2005)

Brokeback Mountain received widespread acclaim following its September 2005 screening at the Venice and Toronto film festivals. It went on to receive Best Picture and Best Director awards from the British Academy of Film and Television Arts, Golden Globe Awards, New York Film Critics Circle, Critics Choice Awards, and Independent Spirit Awards, among many others. Brokeback Mountain is a ground breaking film because it is an emotional love story that deals with the uncharted, mysterious ways of the human heart just as so many mainstream films have before it. The two lovers here just happen to be men. The script was initially considered too controversial for studio film, but eventually financial backing was provided by Focus Features and River Road Entertainment and filming began in mountainous Alberta in May 2004, and was filmed over 80 sites from Fort Macleod (30 minutes from Lethbridge) which provided the backdrop to Mossleigh's St. Thomas Angelican Church which was used for the wedding of Ennis and Alma, and on the Cowley highway where some scenes featuring Jack's 1950 GMC truck were filmed outside the town's fire hall. In the Savory Suite Café on Railway Avenue in the post office building, there is a plaque with 'Brokeback Mountain was filmed here'. The fictional Brokeback Mountain is actually a composite of three mountain sites: the majestic Mount Lougheed near Canmore, and Fortress and Moose mountains in Kananaskis Country.

Stylish Place to Stay

Paintbox Lodge, Canmore
The Paintbox Lodge is an intimate Heritage Style Mountain Inn, the ultimate in romantic ambiance, charm, and elegance, recapturing the glory days of the early 1900s when visitors vacationed in the Canadian Rockies in the most luxurious of rustic quarters. Appealing to luxury loving adventurers drawn to the breathtaking grandeur of the Canadian Rocky Mountains the Inn is conveniently situated town centre, in the quaint mountain community of Canmore.

Delicious Place to Eat

Ranchman's Cookhouse & Dancehall, Macleod Trail
Ranchman's has been a cowboy fixture in Calgary since April 28, 1972. There is no other place so steeped in Alberta's Pioneer Western Heritage, and is home to the professional rodeo cowboy. It's a fun place with a vibrant atmosphere serving big meals such as thick steaks, fall-of-the-bone ribs, and Hearty Texas Chili. It was also featured in Brokeback Mountain, as the country and western bar where Jack Twist meets Lureen.

Genre: Action + Adventure
Destination: Ontario

✦ Regional Information

Ontario is Canada's most populous province, highlighted by the sheer size and energy of its two largest cities (one the federal capital, the other the provincial capital), Ottawa and Toronto. Toronto, in particular, is widely regarded as one of the most vibrant and cosmopolitan cities on the continent, in part due to its huge influx of immigrants and home to the famous Toronto film festival TIFF), which brings glamour to the city. The city has also countless galleries, museums and shops, all against the backdrop of both heritage buildings (such as Old City Hall, built in 1899) and innovative modern architecture (such as the CN Tower).

The far north and west of Ontario is a largely uninhabited wilderness of lakes, swamps and forests. Throughout Ontario are five national parks and 330 provincial parks. And, surreal as it may seem when compared to the province's urban centres, there are parts of this province where you can see more polar bears than humans. Ontario is also a province with plenty of water, and home to the world famous Niagara Falls.

There are many ways to experience Niagara Falls. Get up close and personal, on the classic Maid of the Mist boat. This famous Niagara Falls tour has being taking visitors right up to the base of the Falls since the 1950s. Another way to get close to the Falls is to Journey Behind the Falls. This 30-45 minute tour takes visitors on an elevator 150-feet down through bedrock to tunnels behind the Falls, including an Observation Deck at their base.

From above tourists can get to the Skylon Tower which rises 236 metres above Niagara Falls and offers some of the most spectacular views not only of the Falls but also of the surrounding region including Buffalo, Toronto, and the beautiful Niagara wine region. If that's a little too high, the Konica Minolta Tower Observation Deck, on the 25th storey, also features great views. For those who want an Adrenaline rush, then head straight to Niagara Helicopters or Whirlpool Jet Boat Tours. Niagara Helicopters

takes off every 15 minutes in six-seat helicopters for an unmatched experience of the Falls, while Whirlpool Jet Boat Tours takes visitors on a 1500 horsepower Jet Boat (choose the Wet Jet to feel the water or the Jet Dome to stay dry) into Class 5 whitewaters and the famous whirlpool. As night falls it is just as spectacular as several nights each week, a fireworks display at Queen Victoria Park adds a little extra dazzle.

Ontario has recently been a magnet for film makers too, with the government encouraging film and TV tax credits for a financial incentive, places such as Hamilton have now become very popular. In 2007, the film The Incredible Hulk was filmed on Main Street East — a two-week night shoot that featured the film's climatic fight scene between the Hulk and Abomination. Temporary buildings were erected by the film's crew on parking lots behind the Royal Connaught Hotel building on the north side of Main as well as across the street on the southwest corner of Main and John Streets. In 2000, LIUNA Station reopened the James Street North Canadian National rail station as a banquet hall. In 1996 the station was used for the most expensive film ever made in Canada to that time, the mega budget The Long Kiss Goodnight, which cost $95,000,000.00 to make. Also in 2000, X-Men, featuring Hugh Jackman and Patrick Stewart, shot some of its scenes at LIUNA Station, and parts of Sean Connery's Finding Forrester was filmed inside the gymnasium of Cathedral Secondary School on King Street East and Copps Coliseum arena stands in for Madison Square Garden in the film.

Genre: Action + Adventure
Destination: Ontario

X-Men (2000)

Arguably one of the best known Hollywood blockbusters to film in Toronto is X-Men, filmed at locations across the city and in Ajax, Burlington, Hamilton, Oshawa and Sudbury. Professor Xavier's school for the gifted is really Casa Loma and Roy Thomson Hall . Also, the meeting of world leaders was filmed at Central Commerce Collegiate and the Senate hearings at the Metro Hall Council Chambers. The Distillery Historic District, one of Toronto's most popular filming locations, helped set the scene for the concentration camp.

The opening concentration camp scene, in 'Poland, 1944', used the old Gooderham-Worts Distillery, Mill Street toward the Toronto waterfront, an abandoned complex whose empty warehouses are frequently used as makeshift studios (Chicago, The Long Kiss Goodnight, Mimic, The Recruit and Three Men and a Baby are among many movies shot here). The lowlife bar in 'northern Alberta' where Wolverine (Hugh Jackman) is first discovered cage-fighting is also the old distillery.

'Liberty Island' is actually Spencer Smith Park in Burlington, east of Hamilton, while some of the interior shots of the statue are the Bridgeman Transformer Station. The lair of militant leader Magneto (Ian McKellen) was constructed in a forest clearing at the Greenwood Conservation Area in Hamilton, about 40 miles southwest of Toronto.

'Westchester Railway Station', to which Cerebro traces Rogue (Anna Paquin), and Magneto uses his electromagnetic powers to levitate the police cars, is also Hamilton, the CNR (Canadian National Railway) Station, James Street North, Hamilton, which was also the location of the spectacular shoot-out in The Long Kiss Goodnight.

Stylish Place to Stay

Soho Metropolitan Hotel, Toronto
From Madonna and Guy Ritchie to Jay-Z and P. Diddy, the guest list at the Soho Metropolitan Hotel is quite impressive, just like the hotel. This 89-room boutique property, including its restaurant Senses, recently opened in 2003 and has already received international awards. This place becomes packed out during the week of TIFF (Toronto International Film Festival) with international stars.

Delicious Place to Eat

Lobby Lounge, Toronto
A well-known Toronto hot-spot, the Lobby Lounge attracts local beautiful people as well as celebrities like Woody Harrelson, Scarlett Johansson and Sofia Coppola. This place is also packed during TIFF.

Genre: Action + Adventure
Destination: Ontario

 ## Superman II (1980)

The Superman film series consists of five superhero films based on the DC Comics character of the same name. The films contain storylines such as Superman's origin story, growing up in Smallville, fighting Kryptonian supervillains and Lex Luthor, romancing with Lois Lane, and returning to Earth after a long visit to Krypton. Superman II is the 1980 sequel to the 1978 superhero film Superman. It was the only Superman film to be filmed by two directors

During the film Clarke Kent and Lois lane were sent on an assignment by the Daily Planet to Niagara. While pretending to be on their 'honeymoon' Lois and Clark tour the Falls, Lois sends Clark for refreshments. Meanwhile, a small child accidentally plunges into the Falls but before he can reach the bottom, Superman quickly swoops in and saves the boy. Lois, noticing Clark's absence during Superman's appearance, becomes suspicious that Clark is Superman. She tells Clark of her suspicions and to prove them, throws herself into the water upstream of the Falls, expecting Clark to become Superman to rescue her, but Clark manages to secretly use his heat vision to cut a tree branch into the water, saving Lois by more conventional means. Later in the movie Clark reveals his true identity as Superman in the honeymoon suite, when trips over the pink polar bear rug and 'burns' his hand in the log fire.

 ## Stylish Place to Stay

Marriott Niagara Falls & Spa, Niagara Falls
The Hotel Niagara Falls, where Superman and Lois Lane were posing as a newly married couple doesn't actually exist; but if you have a romantic streak then this hotel will fit the bill. Their Presidential Loft suites have a mini-bar, fireplace and whirlpool tub, all of which enjoy floor to ceiling views of the Falls. Also check out their Niagara Falls romance package that include champagne, breakfast and romantic dining for two, or their honeymoon package with his-and-hers spa treatments.

 ## Delicious Place to Eat

Peller Estate Winery, Niagara Falls
Awarded the highest Zagat rating 'Extraordinary', Peller Estates Winery Restaurant offers sweeping vineyard views, and sumptuous wine and food pairings created by Winery Chef and CityLine personality Jason Parsons that evolve with the changing seasons. Visit this superb winery and taste some of the fine wines they have on offer – they also provide private tours of the vineyards, and 'Barrel Cellar' dinners for something extra special.

Genre: Romantic Comedy
Destination: Quebec

✈ Regional Information

Québec offers perhaps the most complete mix of culture, scenery and wildlife of any of Canada's provinces. It is the second most populous province, after Ontario, and most inhabitants live in urban areas near the Saint Lawrence River between Montreal and Quebec City, the capital. In the Province of Québec, the official language is French, though there are many places within the province where large populations of English speakers can be found, such as in the city of Montréal, and in certain neighbourhoods of Québec City. Even though not everyone in Québec is a native speaker of Québécois French, this province still has, by far, the largest French-speaking population of Canada.

No trip to French-speaking Canada is complete without a visit to romantic Québec City, where 90% of its residents are French speaking. Due to this, most films made and produced here are French, however in most years; the top-grossing Canadian film is a French-language film from Quebec. However English speaking Hollywood movies such as 'The Aviator', and 'Catch me if you can', have been known to have filmed scenes here. There's a definite European sensibility here and you'll feel farther from home then you are, walking down cobblestone streets and stopping in small shops selling everything from pastries and artisanal cheese to antiques and art. By far the best way—and in some places the only way—to explore Québec City is on foot. Top sights, restaurants, and hotels are within or near Old Québec, which takes up only 11 square km (4 square mi). The area is not flat, so walking takes a bit of effort, especially if you decide to walk to the Upper Town from the Lower Town. If you only have a few days here then make sure you stroll the narrow streets of the Quartier Petit-Champlain, visiting the Maison Chevalier and browse at the many handicraft stores. Then on to Place Royale, head for the Église Notre-Dame-des-Victoires, in the summertime there's almost always entertainment in the square.

Montréal is well known for its European charm, which is especially evident in the cobblestone streets of the Old Port. Meander along the river or stroll down St Paul, before stopping for a croissant at celebrated café and bakery, Olive & Gourmando. Feeling un peu fatigué after all your sight-seeing? Take a soothing break in the eucalyptus steam bath at Scandinave les Bains. After some pampering here, you'll be refreshed, relaxed and ready to continue exploring the stunning architecture of this historic area. To get an idea of life in New France during the 18th and 19th Centuries, a walking tour of Old Montreal is a must. A good place to start would be the Notre-Dame-de-Bonsecours Chapel, which is located at the corner of the rue Saint-Paul and rue Bonsecours in the eastern end of Old Montreal. The nearby Bonsecours Market (Marche Bonsecours), built in 1847, is a testament to Montreal's influence in British North America. The building, comprising of a Greek Revival portico, a tin-plated dome and cast-iron columns imported from England, is a good example of that era's Neo-Classical style. Today it houses boutiques and exhibits. There are several companies who offer tours by foot, boat or take one of the lovely trams around the city. Montreal, like Quebec has also been a successful film making destination. The Montreal World Film Festival (WFF), founded in 1977, is one of Canada's oldest international film festivals and the only competitive film festival in North America accredited by the FIAPF. The public festival is held annually in late August in the city. Unlike the Toronto International Film Festival, its counterpart in English-speaking Canada, the Montreal World Film Festival focuses on various kinds of films from all over the world but features few if any produced in Hollywood.

Genre: Romantic Comedy
Destination: Quebec

The Whole Nine Yards (2000)

This film is a story of a dentist from Chicago, living in Quebec, Nicholas 'Oz' Ozeranski (Matthew Perry) is trapped in a miserable marriage to the daughter of his late, ex-partner. He can't divorce her because her father embezzled from the dental practice, and it would leave him with nothing but debt. As well as starring Matthew Perry, the film has quite a star studded cast with Bruce Willis as the infamous killer, Jimmy 'the Tulip' Tudeski and Rosanna Arquette. The film was the first main-stream American movie to be filmed in Montreal. Although the script originally set the story in Miami, both for financial and creative reasons the scenario was moved to Montreal. Production designer David Snyder was one of the first to suggest that Montreal be used not just as a backdrop but to actually incorporate the locale into the script. The filmmakers quickly agreed. "I think in a funny way this film has a sort of French sensibility," says the director. "There's a great tradition in France of funny movies about gangsters, such as 'Borsalino' and 'Shoot the Piano Player,' that have a combination of amorality and sweetness that is more typical of a European than an American picture." Speaking of the film the director adds "Once the story was set in Montreal, we had a fabulous opportunity to shoot the city and take advantage of all the marvellous architecture, the environment and the French signage, we found wonderful settings for each scene that give the film a fresh look for audiences who may not be familiar with this city."

Stylish Place to Stay

The Quebec Ice Hotel, Quebec
Each year the cathedral-like hotel is carved entirely of 15,000 tonnes of ice, including the furniture and even ice candelabras hanging from the 18ft ceilings. Generally, the Quebec Ice Hotel's season is from January to the beginning of April. The walls are 4 feet thick and insulate the hotel to a crisp but comfortable –2° to –5°C. Visitors may choose to just pass through for a tour and a drink at the ice bar or stay overnight.

Delicious Place to Eat

Toqué!, Montreal
When it comes to famous cuisines of Montréal, French food ranks high on the list of favourites. With the French it is all about romance, and presentation, and this place is no exception. Long the king of Montreal's restaurant scene, Chef Normand Laprise works magic with fresh market ingredients and his seared foie gras is legendary. Toqué! won CAA's (and America's AAA) highest award, the five-diamond rating, in 2006, only one of two restaurants in the city to receive this accolade. Reservations are essential - book a month ahead.

Stanley Park

Moonstruck

Dead Man's Island

West End

Wedgewood
Bacchus

To Cannery

Opus

Yaletown

T, Tearoom

Focus On...
Vancouver

Just a two-hour flight from Hollywood, Vancouver has become the third largest centre for the film industry in North America – hence its nickname, 'Hollywood North.' After all, the movie industry pumps $1 billion a year into the local economy, and with flicks like the new Night at the Museum: Battle at the Smithsonian and Twilight: New Moon being shot here, word is out that Vancouver is picking up the glitter of its American Tinseltown sister.

Vancouver has become a hit with movie producers and, by extension, movie stars. This actually isn't a completely new thing. In fact, celebrity lore has tangled with Vancouver since the days when Gary Cooper hitched a ride back to the Fairmont Hotel on a passing street-cleaning machine.

Aside from its obvious outstanding natural beauty, Vancouver has a laid-back charm that makes it one of the most popular Canadian cities to visit. It's hip, trendy and cool.

The best 'boutique' style hotel in town is the snazzy, yet luxurious 'Opus Hotel', located near the Yaletown Marina. If you are looking for a hotel that is happening and hip, without the massive attitude you might find at trend setting hotels, this is probably the place for you.

Even though everyone knows Vancouver runs on coffee, drinking tea has become the latest craze. The quality of tea depends on its growing region, soil, weather, harvesting season and ways of processing. You can see (and taste) the difference at T, a tasting boutique located on the West Side where over 100 varieties and blends of tea from the four corners of the world are available. Travellers can sample whole leaf, premium leaf iced, and whole leaf pyramid teabags. The boutique also sells spa kits including the popular Jetlag AM and PM packs. Moonstruck Tea House, has a vast selection of teas, edible flowers and herbs direct from China's best tea farms. Moonstruck also offers Chinese tea ceremonies for two to four people. For something a little stronger then head to funky Subeez an eclectic venue of dripping candles and gothic décor serving classy cocktails and fine wines. It rates very highly as one of Vancouver's most popular bars.

Vancouver is also one of North America's top dining cities, and the city has anywhere from 2,000 to 5,000 restaurants covering all prices and different cuisines. 'Buy local, eat seasonal' is the mantra of all the best restaurateurs in Vancouver, and they take justifiable pride in the bounty of local produce, game, and seafood available to them. The Cannery is a famous Vancouver landmark with magnificent views of mountains and the harbour, serving superb fresh seafood. The outstanding wine list and the comfortable atmosphere make this place a favourite with locals. Bacchus restaurant and lounge, located in downtown Vancouver, is part of the outstanding boutique hotel Wedgewood. Executive Chef Lee Parsons is one of the city's most talented chefs, evident in the slow-cooked textures and concentrated flavours of the finished plate.

ⓘ Stylish Essentials

General Information

Air Canada
www.aircanada.com
T. +1 888 247 2262

British Airways
www.ba.com

WestJet
www.westjet.com
T. +1 888 937 8538

Hertz
www.hertz.com
T. +1 800 654-3001 in the U.S., or
T. +1 800 263-0600 in Canada

Avis
www.avis.com
T. +1 800 331-1212 in the U.S
and Canada

Dollar
www.dollar.com
T. +1 800 800-4000

Thrifty
www.thrifty.com

Budget
www.budget.com
T. +1 800 527 0700 in the U.S., or
T. +1 00 268 8900 in Canada;

Enterprise
www.enterprise.com
T. +1 800 261 7331

National Car Rental
www.nationalcar.com

Amtrak
www.amtrak.com
T. +1 800 872 7245

VIA Rail
www.viarail.ca
T. +1 888 842 7245

Winter Carnaval
www.carnaval.qc.ca

Yukon Quest
www.yukonquest.org

Canadian Tulip Festival
www.tulipfestival.ca
T. +1 888 465 1867

Stratford Festival
www.stratfordfestival.ca
T. +1 800 567 1600

Calgary Stampede
www.calgarystampede.com
T. +1 800 661 1767

Toronto International Film Festival
www.tiffg.ca

Alberta

Alberta General Information
www.alberta.ca

Tourist information
www.discoveralberta.com

Calgary Tourist Information
www.tourismcalgary.com

Cowboy Trail
www.thecowboytrail.com
T. +1 403 652 7010
E. cowboytrail@telus.net

Alberta Movie Maps
www.albertamoviemaps.com

**Brokeback Mountain film
tour information**
www.findingbrokeback.com

Wild Cave Tour's
www.canadianrockies.net/
wildcavetours
T. +1 403 678 8819

Banff Upper Hot Springs
PO Box 900
Banff, AB T1L 1K2, Canada
www.pleiadesmassage.com
T. +1 403 762 1515

Fairmont Pallister
www.fairmont.com/pallister
T. +1 403 262-1234

Fairmont Banff Springs hotel
www.fairmont.com/banffsprings
T. +1 403 762 2211
E. banffsprings@fairmont.com

**Ranchmans Cookhouse
& Dancehall**
www.ranchmans.com
T. +1 403 253 1100
Open: 16.00–Close
(Last call is at 2.00)

Paintbox Lodge
www.paintboxlodge.com
T. + 1 403 609 0482

The Grizzly Paw
www.thegrizzlypaw.com
T. +1 403 678 9983
Open 11.00–22.00

Ontario

Niagara Falls Tourism Information
www.niagarafallstourism.com

Niagara Falls Information
www.niagarafalls.ca

Toronto Tourist Information
www.toronto.ca

Lobby Lounge
Toronto
www.lobbyrestaurant.com
T. +1 416 929 7169

**Peller Estate Winery,
Niagara Falls,**
www.peller.com
T. +1 905 468 4678
E. info@peller.com

Soho Metropolitan
Toronto,
www.metropolitan.com/soho
T. +1 416 599 8800

Marriott Niagara Falls & Spa
Niagara Falls
www.niagarafallsmarriott.com
T. +1 905 357 7300

Maid of the Mist
5920 River Road, P.O. Box 808
Niagara Falls, ON L2E 6V6
www.maidofthemist.com
T. +1 905 358 5781

Quebec

Information about Montreal
www.ville.montreal.qc.ca

Guided Walking Tours

Old Montreal Ghost Trail
T. +1 514 868 0303

Tram Tours

Balade de Vieux Port
www.quaisduvieuxport.com
T. +1 514 496 7678

Boat Tours

Montreal Harbour Cruises
www.croisieresaml.com
T. +1 514 842 9300

Scandinave les Bains
71 rue de la Commune Ouest
Montréal, QC H2Y 2C6, Canada
www.scandinavemontreal.com
T. +1 514 288 2009

World Film Festival
1432 Rue De Bleury
Montreal, QC H3A 2J1, Canada
www.ffm-montreal.org
T. +1 514 848 3883

Ice Hotel Quebec
www.icehotel-canada.com
T. +1 418 875-4522

Toque!
900 place Jean-Paul Riopelle
www.restaurant-toque.com
T. +1 514 499 2084
Open: Closed Sunday and Monday.
No lunch on Saturdays.

Vancouver

Opus Hotel
www.opushotel.com
T. +1 604 642 6787

T, Tasting boutique
located on the West Side
www.tealeaves.com

Moonstruck Tea House
www.moonstruckteahouse.com
T. +1 604 602 6669

Subeez
www.subeez.com
T. +1 604 687 6107

The Cannery
www.canneryseafood.com
T. +1 604 254-9606

Bacchus restaurant and lounge
www.wedgewoodhotel.com

Slumdog Millionaire, courtesy of Getty Images.

Movie Releases 2010
Future films that might inspire you to travel...

February 2010
Cabin in the words, Dear John, Untitled Bob Marley Documentary, Percy Jackson & the Olympians, Remember me, Valentine's Day, Mardi Gras, A couple of Dicks, The crazies, Hot Tub Time machine,

March 2010
Grown ups, Ramona, Season of the witch, Clash of the Titans, Law abiding Citizen,

April 2010
Crowley, Diary of a Wimpy kid, Furry Vengeance, Mary, Mother of Christ, Date Night, The losers, Nerverackers, Oceans, A nightmare on Elm street, Death at a Funeral, The Expendables, Wall street 2

May 2010
Iron Man 2, Letters to Juliet, Robin Hood, Sex and the City 2

June 2010
Five Killers, Gullivers Travels, The A-Team, The Karate Kid, The Green Hornet, The Twilight saga: Eclipse

July 2010
The Last Airbender, Predators, Despicable me, Inception, Dinner for Schmucks, Salt, The Zookeeper, Beastly, Cats & Dogs, Morning Glory, Hairspray 2, The sorcerer's apprentice

August 2010
The B Team, Jonah Hex, Priest, The lottery ticket

September 2010
Guardians of Ga-Hoole, Warrior, Born to be a star, The Town

October 2010
The Zookeeper, The social network,

November 2010
Harry Potter and the Deathly Hallows, Red Dawn, Megamind, Rapunzel

September 2010
Tron-Legacy, The Green Hornet, The chronicles of Narnia: The voyage of the Dawn Treader

*please note that all of the above film release dates are subject to change. Please check with your local cinema for up and coming film releases

Competition

Left, Edingburgh Tattoo, courtesy of Dreamstime.

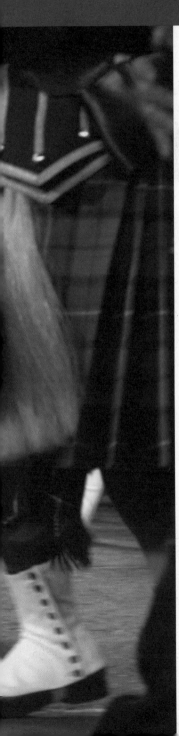

WIN a weekend for 2 to Edinburgh!

Although more commonly known for its castle and cobbled streets, Edinburgh is also famous for the notable celebrities that have been born and raised there. From authors to prime ministers, Edinburgh has been the birthplace of some of the most notable names of the 20th and 21st century.

One of the most famous of these is children's book writer J.K. Rowling. Famed for her Harry Potter series, J.K. Rowling is considered to be one of the most successful writers of recent times. Scenes of the Harry Potter films were also shot around Edinburgh, making use of its beautiful scenery.

Sir Sean Connery is another name to come from Edinburgh; born in Fountainbridge in Edinburgh, Connery is most famous for his cinema role as James Bond. While working as a bodybuilder, Connery gained a part in the stage show South Pacific, eventually leading him on to play James Bond in the film Dr. No in 1962. Since then Connery has starred in seven Bond films, as well as countless other award winning movies throughout his career. In recognition of his contributions to modern cinema, Sean Connery was knighted in July 2000.

Irvine Welsh is another highly successful author to come from Edinburgh. Born in Leith, Irvine Welsh has become internationally famous for his fiction writing, particularly his Trainspotting novel which later became a successful film. From writers to actors, Edinburgh has produced many famous celebrities, and is a popular destination for fans looking to explore the city that has moulded such famous names.

To celebrate the launch of our new book, we are giving away a chance to win a fabulous stylish weekend to Edinburgh for 2 people. The prize includes:

• Accommodation for 1 night @ the Hotel Missoni
• A bus tour of the city's history and highlights
• A tour and tasting session at the Scotch Whiskey Experience
• An indulgent champagne dinner for 2 @ 'The Witchery' restaurant

To enter the competition answer the following question:
Q. What is the name of the New Years Eve party held in Edinburgh?

Email your answer, name and address to ilovefilms@luxurybackpackers.com

Itineraries: inspire your escape

To help you plan your trip or just help you with some inspiration… Luxury Backpackers offer a 'planning & booking' service from a flat fee of £50. We don't charge any commission and we are 100% impartial…. passing on the best advice and best price directly to you. We offer a bespoke service and we can plan anything from a weekend escape to a gap year backpacking.

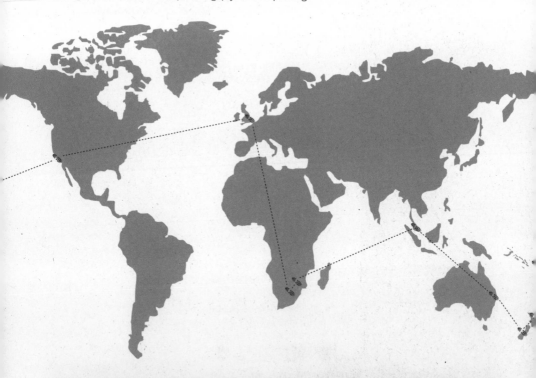

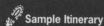 **Sample Itinerary**

London – J'burg – Kruger – Singapore – Sydney – Queenstown – Overland to Christchurch – Overland to Marahau – Overland to Marlborough – Overland to Wellington – Overland to Rotorua – Overland to Waitomo – Overland to Coromandal – Overland to Auckland – Fiji – Los Angeles - London

Economy round the world tickets £2,500

Guidebooks: planning your escape

Buy our other guidebooks in the series!

Visit **www.luxurybackpacker.com**

Acknowledgments

Film Index

A project such as this is a major team effort and relies on the help and generosity of many fantastic people all over the world. Jill & Carlo would like to sincerely thank:

Kerry Dennison, Steve Hall, Max Beesley, Pauline Dennison, Chris (Deluxe Design), Saara Marchadour (The Travel Bookshop), Nicola Osmond-Evans, Stephanie Tomkinson, James Meadows, Carol Farley, Gillian Dewar (VisitScotland.com), Trinh Dang (Fox films), Chanelle Francis (Alliance Films), Louise Taylor (Cheshire Life), Anthony Fabian (Elysian films director), Matilda Pereira (Taj Hotels), Ganesh Krishna (Purple Lotus), Marc Oliva (Angkor Village), Fox Searchlight, and all the support from their friends and family.

Above. Blood Diamond, courtesy of ZML.
Top right. Casino Royale, courtesy of ZML.

ISBN 978-0-9557397-4-3
Published by Luxury Backpackers Ltd 2010 in the UK

Luxury Backpackers Ltd Reg. No. 5661479
Address for Luxury Backpackers can be found on
www.luxurybackpackers.com

Luxury Backpackers, Adventures in Style and the
Luxury Backpackers Logo are trademarks of Luxury
Backpackers Ltd and are registered in the UK Patent
& Trademark Office. Luxury Backpackers Ltd makes
every effort to ensure that all our books and company
stationery are made from 100% recycled paper sources
from post-consumer waste.

Printed in the UK

Designer: Stephanie Tomkinson